PRAYING THROUGH THE

100 GATEWAY CITIES

OF THE 10/40 WINDOW

Edited by
C. Peter Wagner, Stephen Peters & Mark Wilson

P U B L I S H I N G

A Ministry of Youth With A Mission

P.O. Box 55787, Seattle, WA 98155

YWAM Publishing is the publishing ministry of Youth With A Mission. Youth With A Mission (YWAM) is an international missionary organization of Christians from many denominations dedicated to presenting Jesus Christ to this generation. To this end, YWAM has focused it's efforts in three main areas: 1) Training and equipping believers for their part in fulfilling the Great Commission (Matthew 28:19). 2) Personal evangelism. 3) Mercy ministry (medical and relief work).

For a free catalog of books and materials write or call:
YWAM Publishing
P.O. Box 55787, Seattle, WA 98155
(206) 771-1153 or (800) 922-2143

Grateful acknowledgment is made for permission to reprint or adapt the following articles:

"Explaining the 10/40 Window" by Luis Bush, from *The Great Commission Handbook*. Copyright © 1994. Used by permission of Berry Publishing, Evanston, Illinois.

"11,000 Reasons Why Jesus Won't Come Back Yet" by Fred Markert, from *The Last Days Magazine*, Vol. 16.2. Copyright © 1993. Reprinted by permission of Last Days Ministries, Box 40, Lindale, Texas 75771-0040. Additional copies are available from Last Days Ministries at the above address and ask for Ref. #138.

"Intercessors and Cosmic Urban Spiritual Warfare" by Viv Grigg, from *International Journal of Frontier Missions*, Vol. 10.4. Copyright © 1993. Used by permission.

Praying Through The 100 Gateway Cities Of The 10/40 Window

ISBN 0-927545-80-2

Published by YWAM Publishing,
a ministry of Youth With A Mission, P.O. Box 55787, Seattle WA 98155

Cover illustration by Paula Gonzales

Printed in the United States of America

Dedication

To the believers and workers in the 100 Gateway Cities

Contents

Introduction

During October 1993 over 20 million Christians in 105 nations prayed for 62 nations in the 10/40 Window. The result was the largest global prayer initiative in the history of the church. The United Prayer Track of A.D. 2000 & Beyond has designated October 1995 for Praying Through The Window II. The focus for this prayer initiative is the 100 Gateway Cities in 64 nations of the 10/40 Window. Each city is a strategic economic, political, and spiritual center of its respective nation or province (in the case of China and India). It was decided to produce a book of city profiles to facilitate prayer by the 30–40 million intercessors expected to participate, and this volume is the result. Although October 1995 is the designated month for prayer, this guide has been designed for ongoing intercession for the Gateway Cities. The spiritual darkness over these cities makes this initiative not the end, but only the beginning of the battle.

This guide to praying for the 100 Gateway Cities is the product of a global team effort. Workers, many who must remain unnamed because of their sensitive assignments, provided first-hand information on their respective city. Agencies, organizations, and denominations working in the Gateway Cities and 10/40 Window countries also contributed data reflected in these pages. This includes statistics on poverty and the church as well as the prayer points for each city. Such information is what makes this guide so valuable. It is impossible to name each contributor, lest one should be overlooked. However, the worldwide body of Christ thanks each of you, and your labors will be rewarded in heaven.

Acknowledgment must also be given to Patrick Johnstone and his *Operation World*. This valuable resource has been a constant source throughout the preparation of this volume and provided information for prayer points when other information was lacking. Another handy reference has been the outstanding CD-Rom program called *Global Explorer* produced by DeLorme Mapping. We also thank Luis Bush, Fred Markert, and Viv Grigg for permission to reprint their articles. Valuable editorial support has been rendered by Ellen Chappell, Debbie Lee, and Mary Temple. The Caleb Project and the Christian Broadcasting Network have likewise provided important administrative support.

Finally, thanks should be given to the Praying Through the Window II committee who has overseen the production of this volume. Their names and the ministries they represent are: Michael Little, Committee Chairman and President, Christian Broadcasting Network, Virginia Beach, Virginia; Joseph Garlington, Senior Pastor, Covenant Church of Pittsburgh, Pittsburgh, PA; Ted Haggard, Senior Pastor, New Life Church, Colorado Springs, Colorado; Fred Markert, Director of Strategic Frontiers, Youth With a Mission, Colorado Springs, Colorado; Myles E. Munroe, President and Senior Pastor, Bahamas Faith Ministries, International, Nassau, Bahamas; Beverly Pegues, Coordinator, Christian Information Network, Colorado Springs, Colorado; John Quam, National Coordinator, Mission America 2000, Minneapolis, Minnesota; C. Peter Wagner, Professor, Fuller Seminary School of World Mission and Coordinator, A.D. 2000 United Prayer Track, Pasadena, California; Doris Wagner, Executive Director, A.D. 2000 United Prayer Track, Pasadena, California; and John Warton, Jr., Executive Vice President, Luis Palau Evangelistic Association, Portland, Oregon; and Mark Wilson, Coordinator, Christian Broadcasting Network, Virginia Beach, VA.

The Editors

Foreword

Michael Little

In the midst of today's fast-paced and high-tech lifestyle, what a privilege it is to unite in prayer for 100 of the least-evangelized cities! But what is God's heart for the residents who are among the neediest, spiritually and materially, in the world? Most relevant for our day is 2 Peter chapter 3, where God reveals his heart and points to where our hearts as committed believers in the Lord Jesus Christ should be.

Peter's emphasis on the fact of Jesus' return, and how we should then live and think, separates the popular "live for now" temporal values from those that are eternal. Moreover, contemporary translations use a phrase repeated three times in verses 12, 13, and 14— "looking forward"—which speaks of the day he will return and when we, his followers, will be with him.

Peter says that this attitude of increasing expectation should result in a more disciplined spiritual life. But, very significantly, he says in verse 12 that we can actually hasten or "speed its coming," referring to the day of his return.

This is an awesome concept and responsibility—that we could so dramatically influence such an event by our attitudes and actions. But it is consistent with Matthew 24:14, where Jesus says his return is contingent on the fulfillment of the Great Commission:

And this gospel of the kingdom will be preached in the whole world as a testimony to all nations, and then the end will come.

The monumental task of motivating the church to fulfill the Great Commission can be overwhelming. However, Jesus taught us that he is the burden-bearer. It is our duty and privilege to pray and to discuss these overwhelming responsibilities with him. Yet we are to be specific in our prayers.

We are to pray for the harvest workers (Matthew 9:36-38).

We are to pray for the needed changes in ourselves that he wants to accomplish for his purposes (2 Peter 3:14–18).

We are to pray that we will see the world with God's love and compassion, as did Christian statesman Bob Pierce who prayed "to have our hearts broken with the things that break the heart of God."

From our human view the physical means to reach the world is "do-able." The technology exists to penetrate every geographic and political barrier. Shortwave radio has reached around the globe for decades. Satellite delivery of TV signals is now world-wide. CNN television news demonstrates global saturation by being available on satellite over every country on the earth.

The Christian Broadcasting Network, where I serve, now produces and distributes innovative television programs in over 35 languages in 50 nations. Like many other ministries, organizations, and denominations, CBN is committed to evangelizing the whole world. We know the importance of partnerships and enjoy the fruit of many strategic alliances. We can see, then, in the practical realm how "easy" it is to reach all the unreached.

But ours is a spiritual battle, for which prayer is the only answer! With Praying Through the Window II, we are excited to be a part of motivating and inspiring others to pray, especially in October 1995, for the least evangelized cities in the 10/40 Window.

We need focus both in our lives and in our spiritual goals. This prayer initiative sponsored by the United Prayer Track of A.D. 2000 & Beyond gives us that needed focus. It is the committee's desire that this guide will assist you in praying through the 100 Gateway Cities. Thank you for joining us, whether at home or on-site, as we seek God's kingdom to come and his will to be done among the unreached peoples in these strategic cities.

What Is The 10/40 Window?

Luis Bush

The core of the unreached people of our world lives in a rectangular-shaped window! It is a belt that extends from West Africa across Asia, between 10 degrees north to 40 degrees north of the equator. If we are serious about providing a valid opportunity for every people and city to experience the love, truth, and saving power of Jesus Christ, we cannot ignore the reality that we must concentrate on this region of the world which could be termed "the 10/40 Window."

Historical Significance

Why do committed Christians need to focus on the 10/40 Window? First, because of the historical and biblical significance of this part of the world. It was in the 10/40 Window that we encounter the account of Adam and Eve. God's plan for man as expressed in Genesis 1:26 had to do with dominion. Man was to "keep" or guard God's paradise and to have dominion and subdue the earth.

In the book of Genesis, we read the historical account of the fall of man, when Adam and Eve failed to guard God's paradise and forfeited the right to rule over the earth. Then came the flood followed by the building of the tower of Babel, both of which took place in the 10/40 Window. This effort by man to try to rally together in defiance against God resulted in the introduction of different languages, the scattering of the people, and the formation of nations.

Ancient history was worked out in the territory marked by the 10/40 Window, from the cradle of civilization in Mesopotamia across the Fertile Crescent to Egypt. Ancient empires came and went. The fate of God's people Israel rose and fell depending on their obedience to the covenant with their God. Here Christ was born, lived his life, died on the cross, and rose again.

It was not until the second missionary journey of the apostle Paul toward the end of the biblical record, that events of divine history occurred outside of the territory identified as the 10/40 Window. For the committed Christian, the fact that so much of God's dealing with humanity took place on the piece of earth encompassed by the 10/40 Window is a significant reason to focus on it.

Unevangelized Peoples

There is a second reason why committed Christians should focus on the 10/40 Window. While this is only one-third of the earth's total land area, almost two-thirds of the people in the world reside in here. These people live in 64 countries. They include both sovereign states and non-sovereign dependencies. Only those countries with a significant majority of their area lying within the 10/40 Window are included.

When the 55 most unevangelized countries are overlaid upon the countries in the 10/40 Window, we immediately see a very close fit. In fact, 97 percent of the 3 billion people who live in the 55 most unevangelized countries live in the 10/40 Window. This constitutes the core of the challenge of reaching the unreached.

We need to think of the mission of Christ who came to seek and to save the lost, as taught in the parables about the lost sheep and the lost coin. Christ made great efforts to heal, restore, and save just one person. We need to consider Christ's mandate to preach the gospel to every creature, to make disciples of all the nations, and to be his witnesses to the uttermost parts of the earth when we think about those people who live in the 10/40 Window.

The Heart of Islam

A third reason committed Christians need to focus on the 10/40 Window is that it is the heart of Islam. North Africa and the Middle East represent the core of the Islamic religion. Adherents to the Islamic religion are growing, as is suggested by the increased numbers pilgrimaging to Mecca. Yet at the same time, it is reported that many Muslims—having studied the Koran in great depth—have discovered in the process that the highest prophet described in the Koran is Jesus Christ and not Muhammad.

We must pray that just as Eastern Europe recognized that the atheistic ideology of Communism could not stand the test of time, so also the "eyes" and the "hearts" of the Muslims will be opened to the truth.

Three Religious Blocs

A fourth reason to focus on the 10/40 Window is that it's where the three main religious blocs are located. There is the Muslim bloc with 706 million people or 22 percent of the 3.14 billion people living in the 10/40 Window. There is the Hindu bloc with 717 million people or 23 percent of the people living in the 10/40 Window. And there is the Buddhist bloc with 153 million people or close to 5 percent.

On May 6, 1990, the *Jordan Times* in Amman published a report from Algiers titled "Collapse of Communism Will Weaken Islam." In a conference on the future of Islam, Egyptian writer Fahmi Howeidi argued that "the Islamic World is marginalized in a new map." Howeidi was among 40 scholars and political leaders from ten Arab countries attending the conference. He said: "Christianity has been regenerated in Eastern Europe...Changes in Eastern Europe showed that a liberal model of society...based on Christian, capitalist values, was sweeping the world. Islam had yet to come up with a viable alternative."

The Poor

The fifth reason to focus our attention on the 10/40 Window is that the poor are there. In fact, more than 8 out of 10 of the poorest of the poor, who on the average have a gross national product of under $500 per person per year, live in the 10/40 Window. Over one-half of the population of the world lives in poverty with less than an average of $500 per person. Of these people, 2.4 billion live in the 10/40 Window. Despite this fact, only 8 percent of all missionaries work among these people.

In the book *Target Earth*, Bryant L. Myers of World Vision and MARC wrote an article titled "Where are the Poor and

Lost?" Myers suggested that "the poor are lost, and the lost are poor." He arrived at this conclusion after observing that the majority of the unreached live in the poorest countries of the world.

As Christians gathered from some 170 countries at Lausanne II in Manila, there was a heart concern expressed for the materially poor of the world in the second section of the "Manila Manifesto." The document reads, "We have again been confronted with Luke's emphasis that the Gospel is the Good News for the poor (Luke 4:18; 6:20; 7:22) and have asked ourselves what this means to the majority of the world's population who are destitute, suffering and oppressed. We have been reminded that the law, the prophets, and the wisdom books and the teaching and ministry of Jesus, all stress God's concern for the materially poor and our consequent duty to defend and care for them."

There is a remarkable overlap between the 50 poorest countries of the world and the least evangelized countries of the world. In fact, 79 percent of the people who are the poorest are also in the least evangelized countries of the world. And when you relate them to the 10/40 Window you discover that 99 percent of these least evangelized poor—2.3 billion people—live in the 10/40 Window. Only 6 percent of the missionary force now work among this 44 percent of the world's population. This certainly constitutes the greatest challenge of this decade for the committed Christian.

Quality of Life
There is a sixth reason to focus on the 10/40 Window. It relates to the quality of life. One way of measuring the quality of life has been to combine three variables: life expectancy, infant mortality, and literacy. More than 8 out of 10 of the people living in the 50 countries of the world with the lowest quality of life also live in the 10/40 Window. This represents 47 percent of the population, yet only 8 percent of the foreign missionary force works among these people. Over 9 out of 10 of these people live in Hindu or Muslim countries.

The psalmist wrote, "Blessed is the nation whose God is Jehovah" (Psalm 33:12). Certainly, in comparing the relationship of the quality of life in the 10/40 Window with that in those countries which have a higher percentage of Christians, it becomes apparent that the Lord God blesses a nation that turns to him. Yet in turn, he expects the nation who is blessed to be a blessing to other nations as it says in Psalms 67:1-2: "May God be gracious to us and bless us and make his face shine upon us, that your ways may be known on earth, your salvation among all nations."

Stronghold of Satan

Why do committed Christians need to focus on the 10/40 Window? Because it is a stronghold of Satan. The people living in the 10/40 Window have suffered not only hunger and a lower quality of life compared with the rest of humanity, but have also been kept from the transforming, life-giving, community-changing power of the gospel.

The Scripture makes it clear from the writings of Paul the apostle that "the god of this age has blinded the minds of unbelievers, so that they cannot see the light of the gospel of the glory of Christ, who is the image of God (2 Corinthians 4:4).

In the same letter, the apostle writes in 10:3-4, "For though we live in the world, we do not wage war as the world does. The weapons we fight with are not weapons of the world. On the contrary, they have divine power to demolish strongholds." It appears from a careful observation of the 10/40 Window that Satan has established a territorial stronghold with his forces to restrain the advance of the gospel in that territory.

We need to significantly increase our efforts in this decade to reach those who are in the 10/40 Window. If we are to be faithful to Scripture and obedient to the mandate of Christ, if we are to see the establishment of a mission-minded church-planting movement within every unreached people and city by A.D. 2000, if we are to give all peoples a valid opportunity to experience the love, truth, and saving power of Jesus Christ, we must get down to the core of the unreached—the 10/40 Window.

The Challenge of the 10/40 Window

Fred Markert

With your blood you purchased men for God from every tribe and language and people and nation (Revelation 5:9).

Almost every time the Bible mentions the word "nations," it refers not to political countries like France, India, or Australia, but to people groups. Biblical nations are people groups, such as the Serbs in Yugoslavia, the Kurds in Iraq, the Navajo in America, or the Pitjanjara of Australia. It is calculated that there are about 24,000 distinct ethnic groups in the world today.

Matthew 24:14 reflects God's tenacity in accomplishing his central purpose of reaching all nations. "And this gospel of the kingdom will be preached in the whole world as a testimony to all nations, and then the end will come." The original Greek word translated as "nations" here actually means "ethnic groups" or "people groups." A people group is defined as any grouping that has specific characteristics such as geographic location, language, religion, or culture.

How much progress have we made in the past 1,000 years to fulfill God's goal of reaching all people groups? We have reached 13,000 of these groups with the gospel, but 11,000 still have not heard. No matter what your end-time theology, Jesus told us that the end would never come until all peoples have an opportunity to hear the gospel.

A Promise of Blessing

God's goal from the beginning of time was for humanity to fill the earth and rule it while enjoying intimate relationship with him. This ideal situation was shattered when sin entered the world, turning our perfect planet into a raging war zone. Though man purposely turned his back on God, the loving Creator still desired relationship with his creation. All of history is the account of his plan to bring that about—and the story begins with one man.

When God started looking for someone whose heart was

open to him, he was impressed with Abraham. In Genesis 12: 2–3 God promises to Abraham, "I will make you into a great nation...and all the peoples on earth will be blessed through you."

This promise is reaffirmed to both Abraham and Isaac (Genesis 22:18; 26:4), with God making a solemn covenant with Abraham that "through your offspring all nations on earth will be blessed." This blessing would ultimately be fulfilled through Jesus, who came to reconcile all people to God. Jesus was sent to ensure that all peoples would know him.

The 10/40 Window

The part of the globe least touched by the gospel is called "the 10/40 Window." It is an area that roughly spans from 10 degrees latitude north of the equator to 40 degrees latitude north, and stretches from West Africa to East Asia. 95 percent of the unevangelized and 84 percent of the world's poor live there, as well as most of the world's Muslims, Hindus, and Buddhists.

These groups are not masses of faceless people, but individuals whom God loves intimately. He knows the Puku-Geeri-Keri-Wipsi of Nigeria, the Bozos of Mali, the Hwla of Togo, and the The of Laos. He does not want any of them to perish, but all to come to repentance (2 Peter 3:9).

Tragically, most of these people groups have absolutely no access to the gospel. They have no Bible, no Christian literature, no radio or television programs. There is no one to tell them. They will never come to the Lord if no one takes the gospel to them. Yes, we have needs at home, but the only way the Puku-Geeri-Keri-Wipsi will ever hear is if Christians leave home to reach them.

Just the Facts...

The world's population can be divided into three segments:

- • Christian World—that part which has heard the gospel and been influenced greatly by it (1.87 billion people).

- • Evangelized Non-Christian world—that part in which up

to 50 percent of the people have been evangelized, but are still resistant (2.52 billion people).

- Unevangelized world—that part which has never heard the gospel and is often removed geographically, culturally, and linguistically from Christians (1.9 billion people).

Strategy vs. Tactics

A pastor recently asked me, "Why should we dedicate money, people, and prayer to reach the Muslims over in Africa and the Middle East when my city is so needy and so many here don't know Jesus? The Muslims aren't affecting my city." Even though most of us do not have much contact with Muslims, they still have an impact on us. Many of them have a strategy to take over the world, including your city. They are strategizing for the entire planet, while many times we are only tactically considering one battle—the battle for our particular city—out of a vast global war.

If Christians continue to think and operate merely on a local tactical level, we will constantly be on the defensive, reacting to the advances of the enemy instead of setting the pace in the war. We will lose the battle for this generation around the world. However, if we think and act strategically by the power of the Holy Spirit, we will continue to see mighty victories for the kingdom of God. We will see the completion of the Great Commission within our generation.

Thinking strategically, the most obvious priority is to plant the gospel in every one of the 11,000 unreached people groups who have no access to the good news unless someone brings it to them. The focus of our world evangelization strategy must be to plant a strong church among each group that will grow to spiritual maturity and eventually evangelize the whole people group.

In God's promise to Abraham in Genesis 12:2–3, he said, "I will bless you...and all peoples on earth will be blessed through you." God wants to bless you, but he wants to bless 11,000 other people groups through you as well. Whether you are a college student or a construction worker, you can pray, you can give, and you can go.

Open the Blinded Eyes

Paul said, "The god of this age has blinded the minds of unbelievers, so that they cannot see the light of the gospel of the glory of Christ, who is the image of God" (2 Corinthians 4:4). Jesus said, "How can anyone enter a strong man's house and carry off his possessions unless he first ties up the strong man?" (Matthew 12:29).

The battle for souls will not be won merely by raising money and sending people. We can have the best strategies, equipment, and missionaries, but God is the only one who can take the blindness from people's eyes. That happens through unceasing prayer (1 Thessalonians 5:17). In other words, we must continue to pray for our particular assignment from the Lord until we see the victorious results.

Ask Me for the World!

God said, "Ask of me, and I will make the nations your inheritance, the ends of the earth your possession" (Psalm 2:8). The specific, fervent prayers of God's people asking him for the nations by name has been a key element in bringing about this special *kairos* moment around the world.

For years, we have focused our prayers and efforts toward reaching communist Eastern Europe and the Soviet Union. Now we are seeing the answers to all those prayers. Why are tremendous things taking place in Saudi Arabia and Kuwait? During the Persian Gulf War, the families and friends of our soldiers prayed for that area. We started praying, and God began to open the eyes of the people of those lands.

Prayer Words

In the early 1300s, a Frenchman named Raymond Lull developed a burden for the Muslim world, and went to live and preach among the Muslims in Bugia, Algeria. He was the first Christian missionary to the Muslims. After several years, he became the first Christian martyr among the Muslims.

Since 1960 God has led groups of Christians from around the world to go to Bugia for prayer and spiritual warfare. They felt God saying they were not to preach, but to pray. Recently every villager in Bugia became a Christian after Jesus appeared to each of them in dreams on the same night. The spiritual "soil" had been prepared through prayer, their blindness was lifted, and the kingdom of God was able to advance and plunder the strong man's household.

But Only If We Do It

Why are the nations of Senegal, Bhutan, Chad, and Azerbaijan so resistant to the gospel? Because many of us have never heard of them, so we have not been praying for them—their eyes are still blinded by the god of this age. If we are going to be part of what God is doing in the world today, we need to pray specific prayers. You can get in on the excitement of this *kairos* harvest by adopting one of these Gateway Cities for daily prayer, not stopping until it is reached with the gospel. James 5:16 declares that "the prayer of a righteous man is powerful and effective." We may not be able to see the results of our prayers right away, but God has promised that they will be effective.

Putting Our Treasure Where God's Heart Is

If we understand the priority of reaching the unreached peoples in the cities, it will show in our giving as well as in our praying. But research shows that the majority of born-again Christians do not tithe regularly. We are not contributing as much or as wisely as we should.

• Christians give $157 billion annually to churches and mission agencies. Of that, 94 percent is used in the Christian world, 5.5 percent in the Evangelized Non-Christian world, and only 0.5 percent to the Unevangelized world.

• We sponsor 308,000 missionaries who work outside the United States. Of those, 90.0 percent work in the Christian world, 8.1 percent in the Evangelized Non-Christian world, and only 1.1

percent (3,400 people) are working to reach the 1.19 billion in the Unevangelized world.

• Of the $3 billion spent annually to sponsor television and radio programs, 99.9 percent is used in the Christian world, .09 percent in the Evangelized non-Christian world, and only .01 percent in the Unevangelized world.

This does not mean we should stop giving money to our churches or to the ministries we know and support. But we need to be good stewards. This means we need to increase our giving to frontier missions, as well as reviewing carefully where our current donations are being used. The Bible says in 1 Samuel 30:24 that "the share of the many who stayed with the supplies is to be the same as that of him who went down to the battle. All will share alike." Whatever your part in the Great Commission, you will have the same reward as those on the front lines.

Carpe Aeternitas

In 23 B.C., the Roman poet Horace penned a phrase that has become the battle cry of modern secular man, *"Carpe Diem. Quam minimum credula postero"*— "Seize the day. Put no trust in the morrow." We in the church need to take up as our battle cry, *"Carpe Aeternitas"*—"Seize eternity!"

We can do this by praying for the Gateway Cities and the unreached people groups in them by name, by making sure our resources are being used wisely, and by going, either short-or long-term. God has thrust the battle upon us by releasing this remarkable season of harvest. Each of us must play our part as a soldier of the cross (2 Timothy 2:3–4) in this crucial hour. Let us rise to action today so we do not look back on this *kairos* season tomorrow with regret for what could have been!

Spiritual Warfare and the Poor in the Gateway Cities

Viv Grigg

This morning my friend, a political leader in exile from an Asian city, told me that the Lord had spoken to him to destroy the prostitution trade in his city. I wept to myself in the quiet of my office. For eight years I had waited for God to answer prayer and raise up such a man.

By A.D. 2000 there will be over 400 cities over 1 million, and over 300 of these could be classified as unevangelized. Some 30-90% of the people of each city live in slums, shantytowns, and squatter areas. As data comes in from around the globe, we find churches in most of these cities. But few have sufficient numbers of believers and churches to effectively evangelize their city. For many years it has been a privilege to walk with my family behind the Lord in the dark side of the mega-cities slums of the third world and to intercede for many of these cities.

Today we are moving towards the fourth era of the modern missions movement—reaching the cities. In the last decade over 1 billion people have careened down rural roads into multiplying concrete highways to be disgorged into the city and its slums. Almost all population increase in the next decades will be both urban and urban migrant, as rural population growth will remain static. The majority of people will be in the slums and squatter areas. The penetration of the cities and these urban poor communities define the target of missions for the next decades. The future of missions is urban, and especially among the poor.

Jesus: Incarnational Intercessor
Given the contexts of massive urbanization, globalization, and impoverishment of city populations, what is our goal in praying? Let us look to the Master to find the answers.

He came preaching the kingdom of God. Preaching, teaching, healing, and delivering were his primary activities. He trained his disciples in the same central issues. *We are to pray for labor-ers for the harvest who can do the same (Matthew 9:37-38).* In Luke 4:18 he declares the focus of his mission and ours is to preach good news to the poor. Spiritual warfare involves entering into the poverty of the poor, for that was the model of him who now intercedes for us.

The Cost of Spiritual Penetration

He had been a language helper for a foreign man of God. One day he refused to give money for the *puja,* the celebration of worship of the goddess. "I have been reading this holy book and it says we are to have only one God." Then he fled from the *bustee* (slum). He gave his life to the one and only God. During those days a train smashed into the community; two houses caught on fire. The people said it was because he had turned against their goddess— perhaps it was, for they would know. The brother to whom he taught language was a man of prayer, and in prayer God spoke to him to take flowers and fruit to the families of those hurt by these events. As he did the people saw God come among them.

This is how the first slum in another city was penetrated with the gospel. What was the cost of initial penetration? One worker lost her hearing, another her health. Fifteen workers gave from three to seven years of their lives with severe sicknesses and frequent demonic activities surrounding them. And behind it, several hundred people were praying regularly. Today in ten slums there are emerging groups of worshipping people. And what will be the cost in the next city? Somebody might have to give 15 to 20 years of his or her life for this people, building upon the initial penetration. Every step must be bathed in prayer by hundreds of intercessors.

High Intensity Intercessory Warfare

Not only demographically but theologically the final arenas of con-flict will be battles within cities: between the bride of Christ, God's people as the city of God, and biblical Babylon, which represents the emerging international network of cities—the global city itself.

The casualties will be great. The level of direct confrontation with the powers will be more intense. George Otis, author of *Last of the Giants*, highlights the strategic place of Iraq (Babylon) and Iran (the kingdom of Persia) in the biblical end-time scenarios, as being strongholds of two immensely powerful spirits.

But there are other centers of tremendous power in the 10/40 region. Calcutta is the center of Kali and Brahmanic Hinduism; Varanasi is one of India's holiest Hindu strongholds. Lhasa has its mysterious Buddhist powers, and towards Mecca one-fifth of the world's population prays daily. Penetrating these cities will be hard, persecution will be intense, and workers might face death. Powers are centered in the Gateway Cities, control countries or whole regions, and seek to extend their influence over the whole earth.

At the same time as we face a higher level of intensity of spiritual opposition, the world is moving into cities. Here the depravity of man creates grotesque structures that enable the spiritual powers to wreak great destruction in increasing levels. And so in general, reaching and transforming the cities becomes increasingly difficult.

Covenant Cities

Taking cities has to do with reestablishing the covenants of the cities, destroying the covenants made with devils, and reestablishing covenants with God.

The first city was built by Cain in rebellion against God (Genesis 4:17). His descendants went on to build Babylon (Genesis 11:4–9). In the Scriptures Babylon begins as the name of a city but takes on the meaning of a principality far larger than any city. It represents a world urban system covenanted against God. In a similar manner, Jerusalem comes to represent not just the geographical location of the city of God, but a picture of the universal city where God dwells—a covenant city.

Today in the same manner, we find Bangkok, the "city of the angels." In regular daily ceremonies, every portion of its land is dedicated to the spirits, for whom small houses are constructed.

Kalikata, or Calcutta, is named after a goddess. This city of death is a servant of the goddess of death and destruction. Discernment of these spiritual powers helps in preparation for the battle. Both discernment and battle occur by the preaching of the word, the word of our testimony, the signs that follow, and "loving not of our lives unto death."

While the concept of principalities dwelling over territories may be inferred from the Scriptures, the Word indicates that the primary biblical categories are not simply geographical thrones and dominions but the warfare is against the philosophies and religions of the people. Frequently powers are "isms" that have a territorial center. For example, Hollywood has been the name not only for a place but for a demonic intrusion into the homes of millions, propagating licentiousness, adultery, and immorality as well as undermining many forms of restrictions on human sexual practices that are necessary for holding the family together.

Through the proclamation of the gospel, the kingdom impacts the very structures of cities. The Scriptures are also consistent that working for justice in society is both part of a righteous person's lifestyle and lays the basis for intercession. Colossians 1:15-20 tells us that Christ is above all things and in control of the structures of the universe. He holds cities together.

Strategic Issues in Intercession

1. Finding God's Plan for a City
For each city God has a purpose. And for each city God has a battle plan. It is our task to discern it and then to walk with him in obedience. Listening, unity, and timing are crucial factors. Every step in finding God's plan is the working of the Spirit, as we work with him. Every city is different and will follow a different pattern with a different time frame and style. Every battle is different.

2. Spiritual Unity—the Key to Spiritual Warfare
Linking believers around a common goal is a central element of reaching a city. This must be birthed by the Holy Spirit. The spiri-

tual unity of believers is a key to spiritual power (see Acts 4:32–35). The Holy Spirit may not work significantly in a situation where he is grieved due to disunity.

3. Theology of Brokenness

If there is not significant unity, the first step is to bring together the believers in prayer or in renewal and teaching until there is reconciliation and brokenness. The riots in Los Angeles, for example, were the key to catalyze the brokenness of that city's church. After the riots Koreans, Hispanics, Afro-Americans, and Anglos publicly confessed their sins to each other and began to work on issues of transforming the city together.

4. Prayer Movements

Prayer births visions of what God can do in the city and builds mutual trust and relationship. It is a common denominator around which many diverse Christian groups can work in unison. Citywide prayer, prayer walks, prayer marches, neighborhood prayer strategies, and concerts of prayer are some of the components of such movements of prayer.

5. Release From Worldly Powers

Many sins prevent effective intercession, and some stand out. Penetrating urban centers of affluence may require the voluntary renunciation of wealth. St. Francis of Assisi, wealthy as a young man, has been the universal model of apostolic poverty. It was his release from the powers of greed that enabled him to move into levels of spiritual power and save whole cities.

6. The First Issue in Spiritual Authority

Out of our sufferings God gives a level of authority for part of the warfare in a city. Jesus gave an absolute principle that "unless the grain of wheat dies it does not bear fruit." He modeled it, for "Jesus became a man and dwelt among us." Incarnation among the poor releases the power of the Spirit. To choose suffering with the poor produces the character of the Spirit, enabling an outflow of his power.

7. Reaching the Poor

From the ministry of preaching among the poor emerge spiritual leaders for the city. Being among the poor proves to be a training ground for understanding the structures of the city, which oppress the poor and cause poverty. Luke 4:18 tells us that God unleashes his Spirit especially on such servants.

8. People Group Thinking

The warfare for the unreached peoples of the world will largely be fought in the cities. Unreached people groups have been moving to the cities for mainly economic reasons. Cities have become one of the natural entrance points for missionaries seeking to work with different peoples. Citywide thinking is required to reach cities. Part of this is to develop an analysis of the people groups in each city. But while cities have linguistic groups and ethnic communities, they also have economic groups and class networks, castes, and many other forms of social groups. Diversity of approach is the way to urban evangelization.

Finishing the Mission

The resources to reach the cities with the message of the kingdom of God are available. The potential workers are available. Presence among the poor, proclamation with power, and prevailing prayer remain the keys to bring about closure to the Great Commission and to bring about a discipling movement in every major sector of the Gateway Cities. We need to move from penetration to church planting to movements of transformation of these cities, and this before the Lord returns. Mobilized, focused, informed, trained, and incarnational intercession in Praying Through the Window II is one starting point.

Prayer Journeys to Gateway Cities

C. Peter Wagner

In the decade of the 1990s God has been surfacing a concept which, at least for me, is invigoratingly new. A few have been practicing it for a while, but now God is showing the whole body of Christ how to pray *in* the community.

Concerts of Prayer, Prayer Summits, city prayer alerts, and many other similar activities are designed to promote prayer essentially *for* the city. For example, I belong to a movement called "Love L.A." in which the pastors gather three times a year from 7:00 a.m. to 11:00 a.m. for unity prayer in Hollywood Presbyterian Church and then occasionally in South Central Los Angeles at Crenshaw Christian Center where all believers are invited. From 400 to 1200 pastors have attended, and up to 8,000 lay people have gathered together for prayer. In "Love L.A." we pray *for* our city.

Praying in the City

For some time I had been feeling in my spirit that God was trying to show us something new. Not that the old was bad or that it should be phased out. Quite the contrary, our prayers for the city need to be multiplied in frequency and intensity. It is not either/or; it is both/and.

This is so important to me that I shall not soon forget that I was in a church growth conference in Second Baptist Church Houston in the spring of 1992 when I heard Jack Graham, pastor of Prestonwood Baptist Church of Dallas, verbalize exactly what I sensed God had been showing me:

Revival will come when we get the walls down between the church and the community.

We live today in a time of unprecedented spiritual harvest that promises to increase in the years to come. Jesus said our first response to a ripe harvest is to pray (see Matthew 9:37–38). If we don't pray, the harvest will pass.

Evangelizing the world and our own communities is out-and-out spiritual warfare. Prayer is the major weapon God has given us to fight this battle.

Many kinds of prayer are mentioned in the Bible, and all are important. One of them is warfare prayer, or "binding the strong man." Jesus tells us that when a strong man is overcome, he releases his goods, namely unsaved souls (see Luke 11:20–22).

How do we do this? In warfare prayer, it is most important to move the focus of our prayer outside the walls of the church and into the community.

I was deeply stirred in my spirit when I heard Jack Graham's powerful word. It has become what I believe to be a prophetic word for the body of Christ as a whole. Much of what God desires to do in our cities in the 1990s will happen if we obey this word, and conversely much of what God desires will *not* happen if we fail to obey.

I love the way Jack Graham said it: *"Revival will come...."* Revival only comes. We do not produce or generate it. God sends revival by his Holy Spirit.

But there is a condition: *"When we get the walls down between the church and the community."* God is not going to bring those walls down himself. He could do so by his sovereign power, but he has chosen not to. I imagine one of the reasons might be that he did not put them up in the first place. It is up to us to get those walls down.

Exciting Ways to Pray

Not only has God told us to move our prayers into the community, but he has also given us some exciting and innovative ways to do it. Furthermore, they are fun! Prayer that is fun is a fairly unusual concept, but I believe God is fulfilling for us what Paul wrote to the Philippians: "For it is God who works in you both to *will* and to do his good pleasure" (Philippians 2:13).

There are four ways of praying in the community which have surfaced as principal Christian activities for the 1990s. More may be forthcoming, but these are now in place:

1. *Praise Marches.* These are focused primarily on cities.

2. *Prayerwalks.* These are focused primarily on neighborhoods.

3. *Prayer Expeditions.* These are focused primarily on regions.

4. *Prayer Journeys.* These are focused primarily on strongholds.

A scripture which I sense is a prophetic word for praying outside of our churches today is Joshua 1:3, given by God to Joshua as he was preparing to lead the people of God into the Promised Land. God said, *"Every place that the sole of your foot will tread upon I have given you."*

Through this I believe God is nudging us outside of our churches and physically into our communities to pray there. As we obey him, we will be getting nearer and nearer to the revival he desires to send.

In obedience to God, the A.D. 2000 United Prayer Track has designated one month per year as an all-out effort of the universal body of Christ to pray *in* our communities. We want to get the soles of our feet out on as regular a basis as possible. In October 1993, 257 prayer journey teams traveled into the 62 nations of the 10/40 Window to pray "on site with insight" for one week each. In June 1994 the "Day to Change the World" saw over 12 million believers from all peoples, tongues, and nations on the streets in Marches for Jesus in every time zone of the globe.

Marches for Jesus will continue every year from now on, most of them being on the Saturday preceding Pentecost Sunday on the liturgical calendar.

October will be the designated annual month for other prayer emphases of the United Prayer Track. In October of 1995 a number of prayer journey teams totaling 100 intercessors each will pray (25 per week) in the 100 Gateway Cities of the 10/40 Window. Never before in history have 10,000 intercessors moved to pray behind enemy lines in such a coordinated and informed fashion. What are these prayer journeys?

Prayer Journeys

The devil is very jealous of making sure that the strongholds he is currently using are securely maintained. Prayer journeys are a direct, overt threat to the enemy's well being, and he will do everything possible to oppose them. I say this not to instill fear because "greater is he that is within us than he that is in the world," but I say it to encourage an appropriate degree of caution.

To conduct an intercessory prayer journey, a given church or ministry recruits a prayer team of, say, five to ten members, and sends them to another city or other strategic point for the purpose of on-site prayer. Let's look at an example:

The Asian Outreach ministry in Hong Kong recently sent a team of four intercessors to Danang, Vietnam for a prayer journey. When they disembarked from their 30-hour train ride, they had no specific plans. But they did have a purpose. "We had come to Danang with one specific goal in mind," says Cao An Dien, one of the intercessors. "We had come here to pray." She says that they did not know where in Vietnam the Lord would lead them when they left Hong Kong, but "as we prayed for the cities of Vietnam, we sensed a darkness about Danang, as if there was something significant to pray about."

As they began exploring and looking for prayer targets the first day, they stopped for breakfast in a small restaurant. The restaurant's chef, a Chinese Vietnamese named Trung, told them that he was holding down three jobs so that he could save enough money to escape Vietnam. They didn't have a chance to present the gospel to him, but they did pray for him often while they were in Danang. They prayed for the city, they prayed against the strongholds they could discern, they prayed for the 67 unreached people groups in Vietnam, they prayed for the persecuted Christians there, and they prayed for the individuals they encountered day by day.

Eight months later they were thrilled when one of their team who was ministering in a Vietnamese camp back in Hong Kong ran into Trung! She then shared the gospel with him and left him a devotional book in English and Chinese. Six months later they found him again. This time he was radiant. "I have become a Christian," he beamed. "Through reading this devotional book I have come to know Jesus as my Lord and Savior."

And Danang? Did the prayer journey have an effect? Cao An Dien says, "In the months following our visit there, it was reported that the church in Danang was discovering greater freedom since the government was no longer clamping down as they had before. Many were being saved in this city." Then she adds something very important for prayer warriors to keep in mind: "The Lord was answering not only our prayers but also those of many others who were upholding this city in prayer."

The cost of sending 400 or more teams of up to 25 each to Southeast Asia and North Africa, to India and the Middle East, to Japan and other 10/40 Window destinations is considerable. And this raises a very interesting question for church and ministry leaders: how important is prayer for effective evangelism? Most Christian leaders will say, "Prayer is number one," but much of this turns out to be mere rhetoric. Nothing demonstrates people's real level of commitment more than their willingness to commit money. Depending on many factors, it could cost a church between $10,000 and $25,000 to send an intercessory prayer team to the 10/40 Window.

Those who volunteer for an intercessory prayer journey must realize that they are not going on a vacation. It will not be a week or ten days of sightseeing and shopping. It will be an authentic venture in short-term cross-cultural missions. One advantage is that journeyers will not have to learn a language because they can pray in their native tongue. But in many cases the food will be substandard, they will be plagued by nuisance illnesses such as diarrhea and colds, jet lag will throw their systems out of kilter, accommodations in some cases will be Spartan with few comforts of home. And since this is overt spiritual warfare, challenging areas of deep and long-standing demonic entrenchment will inevitably bring casualties. It is not a job for the fainthearted, but for those few who are called, strengthened and empowered by the Almighty God.

The results can be radical changes in the balance of power in the heavenlies and an outpouring of the kingdom of God in lands and cities previously enslaved to darkness.

Key to the Profiles

Each of the 100 profiles follows a similar format to pack the maximum information into a limited space. The following explanation will enable you to use this information most effectively. When information for a category is unavailable, "unknown" is inserted.

Pronunciation Key: Under each city name is its English pronunciation derived from the *Oxford American Dictionary*. The pronunciation key from this dictionary is utilized throughout. Two distinctives of this key are (1) long "i" is shown as a capitalized "I" and (2) emphasized syllables are highlighted in bold.

Day: City's scheduled day for prayer on the monthly calendar.

Meaning: The meaning of the city's name.

Country: City's country and province, if applicable. An asterisk* identifies the city as a national or provincial capital.

Population: 1995 estimate based on the research of Viv Grigg and Leland Brown for the A.D. 2000 Cities Network.

Religious Breakdown: Statistics are approximate and may not add up to 100%. However, they do illustrate the major religious groups active in the city as well as the strength of Christianity. Statistical data on the individual Chinese cities was largely unavailable, so country-wide statistics were used instead. Although these are not exact, they represent a generally true picture of the state of religion in China today. Christian percentages represent the total number who claim to be Christians. Evangelicals represent those who affirm personal faith in Jesus Christ, regeneration by the Holy Spirit, and the inspiration of the Bible as the basis for Christian living. (For a more comprehensive definition, see "Appendix 5" in *Operation World*, pages 653–54.)

Status of the church: Estimates of in-city churches and/or believers. Believers are classified as either indigenous (national) or expatriate (foreign).

Major Religious Sites: The identification of these sites was primarily supplied by the Sentinel Group with the assistance of Mike McCausland and Charlie Sturges. The Sentinel Group has compiled a more comprehensive list of these power points in the book *Strongholds of the 10/40 Window* by George Otis, Jr., also published by YWAM Publishing.

City Significance/History: A synopsis of the city's history and significance is provided. Further information can be found in travel guides, encyclopedias, and gazetteers.

Prayer Points: These are specific areas for prayer requested by in-city believers and workers. Each point is an excellent place to start in praying for the city. Additional information can be found in newspapers, magazines, missions periodicals, and prayer letters.

Geographical Sections: The profiles of the 100 Gateway Cities are divided into four geographical sections. These divisions are arbitrary and for organizational purposes only. *Operation World*, for example, places some of the 10/40 Window countries into different regions.

Unreached Peoples: At each sectional break the leading unreached people groups are listed with their respective city. This list was developed by John Gilbert of the Unreached Peoples Resource Network under the direction of its coordinator, John Robb.

Northern Africa

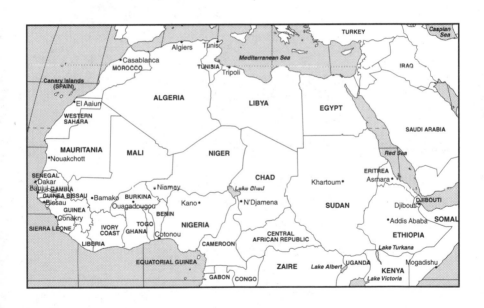

21 Cities

CITY	MAJOR UNREACHED PEOPLES
Casablanca	Moroccan Arab, Shilha Berber, Riffian, Arabized Berber
El Aaiun	Arab, Arabized Berber, Tahelhait Berber, Tamazight Berber
Nouakchott	Moor, Berber
Dakar	Wolof, Fulakunda, Tukulor, Serer
Banjul	Mandinso, Fula, Wolof, Jola
Bissau	Balanta, Manjako, Fulu, Mande
Conakry	Fula Jalon, Maninka, Susu, Yalunka
Bamako	Bambara, Fula Macina, Malinke, Tuareg, Bozo
Ouagadougou	Southern Senufo, Ivorian Malinke, Mossi, Tuareg
Algiers	Kabale Berber, Algerian Arab, Mozabite Berber, Hamayan Bedouin
Tunis	Tunisian Arab, Sahel Bedouin
Tripoli	Libyan Arab, Tripolitanian Arab, Cyrenaican Arab, Berber
Cotonou	Fon, Yoruba, Aja, Gun
Niamey	Zerma, Hausa, Sokoto Fulani
Kano	Hausa, Toroobe, Kanuri, Fulani
N'Djamena	Shuwa, Fula, Teda, Tubu
Khartoum	Beja, Guhayna, Gaaliin, Eastern Nuer
Djibouti	Issa Somali, Afar, Arab
Addis Ababa	Arusi Galla, Somali, Amhara, Tigrinya
Asmara	Tigrinya, Tigre & Mensa, Arab, Afar
Mogadishu	Somali, Sab, Digil, Rahanwiin

Casablanca
(kas-uh-**blan**-kuh)

Day 1

Meaning: "white house"
Country: Morocco*
Population: 3,858,000
Poverty: Slums and unemployment
Religious Breakdown:
  99.8%   Muslim
  0.15%   Christian
  0.01%   Evangelical
Status of the church: A few
  indigenous churches
Major Religious Sites:
  Hassan II Mosque (one of the world's
  largest mosques), Chleuh Mosque,
  Grand Mosque

City Significance/History:

The modern city of Casablanca originated from an ancient Berber hamlet called Anfa. Phoenician traders also used this site as a North African port.

Islam is deeply rooted in the culture of Morocco. Most Moroccans firmly identify with Islam even if they do not practice their religion. They proudly make their confession of faith: "There is no God but Allah, and Muhammad is his prophet." Devoted and nominal alike have an unquestioning faith in what they have been told and believe Islam is the only true faith.

At the beginning of the century, the French chose the small village of Casablanca for their economic center. The French protectorate lasted from 1912-1956. Today with a population of almost four million, it is by far Morocco's largest, most industrialized and most modern city.

Drawn by economic opportunities, both Arab and Berber migrants from around the country continue to pour into Casablanca. Most of these migrants, fresh from the countryside, are entering a completely different culture from the isolated rural villages.

Prayer Points

1. Pray that people from all language groups would be able to hear the gospel.

2. The few believers mistrust each other and fear that the other will turn them in to the government. This fear hinders believers from meeting together and growing. Pray for unity and koinonia in the Holy Spirit.

3. Pray for increasing numbers to tune their radios to the broadcasts and that Casablancans receiving Bible correspondence materials will not be harassed.

4. Pray that the king and the government would recognize the indigenous church, and that Moroccan church planters would be raised up.

5. Pray for missionary work to be permitted again, and for tentmakers to be called.

El Aaiun
(el I-yoon)

Meaning: "water source"
Country: Western Sahara*
Population: 186,000
Poverty: Over 150,000 Sahrawis live in
   refugee camps in Algeria
Religious Breakdown:
  99.8%   Muslim
  0.16%   Christian
  0.01%   Evangelical
Status of the church: A small underground
   fellowship
Major Religious Sites:
   Central Mosque,
   Citadel and Mosque (at nearby Smara)

City Significance/History:

This oasis was little more than a small village until the Spanish developed an administrative, military, and provincial center some 50 years ago. They were seeking to control their interest in the raw materials of Western Sahara, mainly ore.

Western Sahara, located just south of Morocco, is a disputed territory. Morocco has been fighting for control of the land since Spain relinquished it in 1975.

In addition, a referendum has been proposed by the United Nations that would allow the original inhabitants, the Sahrawis, to decide if they want to be independent as the Saharan Arab Democratic Republic. The republic would be governed by the Polisario Front, an 18 year-old guerrilla movement.

Although there is no official capital in this disputed territory, El Aaiun is the political center of the country. It also serves as an export center for phosphates from the Boukra mines.

It is from here that the Moroccan government administers most of their Western Saharan affairs. Mauritania to the south also has interests in this land.

Disputed Territory

═══ Prayer Points ═══

1. The gospel has never been proclaimed to the Sahrawi people. Pray that it may be preached to them and that the Sahrawis will respond positively to Jesus.

2. Pray that food and medical relief in the name of Jesus may be administered to the Sahrawis suffering in exile.

3. Pray for protection over the small group of Christians who must meet secretly.

4. Pray for the Moroccan Christian converts who have relocated to the city because of job opportunities.

5. Pray for the success of Christian radio broadcasts into the city.

6. Pray that the people may determine their own government and that the unstable political situation may be resolved.

Nouakchott

Day 1

(nwahk-**shot**)

Meaning: "place of the winds"
Country: Mauritania*
Population: 650,000
Poverty: 66% of the people
live in slums
Religious Breakdown:
   99.7% Muslim
   0.26% Christian
   0.01% Evangelical
Status of the church: A small
persecuted church
Major Religious Sites:
   Ministry of Islamic Orientation,
   Boutilimit Home (nearby pilgrimage site)

City Significance/History:

Due to its coastal locale and mild climate, this small village of adobe huts was chosen to be the capital of the Islamic Republic of Mauritania in 1960. By 1964 the population (12,300) started to grow and has dramatically increased in the last 30 years.

In Mauritania, a major ethnic line has been drawn. To the north, Arab/Berber Africans make up the majority of the population, and in the south, black Africans live.

Northern and southern Africans are being forced from the sahel, the region on the edge of the Sahara Desert, because the ever-enlarging Sahara is drying the sahel, depleting its water sources. Storms blow sand forming dunes that cover the fragile drought-stricken land. Therefore, cities like Nouakchott have to support a fast-growing refugee population.

On the city limit, residents of cardboard shantytowns now make up two-thirds of the total metro population. Overpopulation is causing great deforestation which, in a short time, will result in desertification. Their goats, camels, and cows seek survival in the piles of trash. The desert, with sandstorms 200 days a year, now blows on the streets of Nouakchott, one of the newer capitals in the world.

══ Prayer Points ══

1. Pray that Islamic *sharia* law would be overturned and for freedom of religion.

2. Pray for believers to be strengthened in the face of persecution and possible death. Pray for steadfast, godly leaders to be raised up.

3. Pray for Muslims to convert to the truth of Jesus. They face the death sentence, so much grace and courage is needed to follow the Lord.

4. Pray that Christian humanitarian relief to the drought-stricken would show God's love and that the physical needs of the poor would be met.

5. Pray for radio broadcasts in Hassaniya (one of the ethnic peoples) Arabic to be produced. Pray for the translation of a Hassaniya Bible and that the 28% literacy level can be raised so people can read it.

Dakar
(dah-**kahr**)

Day 1

Meaning: "tamarind tree"
Country: Senegal*
Population: 1,847,000
Poverty: Slums and many
   seasonal migrants
Religious Breakdown:
  91.0%   Muslim
  3.6%   Traditional Religions
  5.4%   Roman Catholic
  0.07% Evangelical
Status of the church: Only a few of
   the ethnic groups have churches
Major Religious Sites:
  Grand Mosque

City Significance/History:

Many of the capital cities in Africa were developed by European ruling powers almost 200 years ago. At this time, African seaport cities became important economic centers, trading everything from peanuts to slaves.

Dakar has the most strategic location of them all. It was from Goree Island that 3 million slaves were shipped. As the westernmost point in Africa, Dakar is the best departure port for South America, making it a strategic military location for the Atlantic south of the equator, and a trade hub for West Africa.

Founded by the French in 1857, Dakar was named the capital of French West Africa. This beautiful city is economically wealthy compared to the rest of the country. As the national railway terminus, it fosters significant trade and revenue.

Many poor villagers come to the city to sell vegetables and fruits, or move there in hopes of making money to send back to the village. A missions strategy has developed from this kind of migration. By reaching large, significant cities it might be possible to reach all the ethnic groups in the whole country. If one of these migrants hears the good news of Jesus, he or she might take Jesus back to the village.

══ Prayer Points ══

1. Pray for workers to evangelize the many ethnic communities living in the city. Most of these communities need separate church planting efforts because they speak different languages.

2. Pray for continued religious tolerance by the Muslim government. The freedom to witness without fear of persecution is rare in Muslim countries.

3. Pray that a spiritual breakthrough can occur among the powerful Sufi brotherhoods, who are some of the more fundamentalist Muslims in the country.

4. Pray that the lifestyle of the nominal Christians would be transformed to reflect better a life in Christ.

5. Pray that young people who have moved to Dakar for education and employment would be reached with the gospel. Pray for students at Dakar University.

Banjul
(bahn-**juul**)

Meaning: "bamboo island"
Country: Gambia*
Population: 560,000
Poverty: Subsistence living
for many
Religious Breakdown:
95.4% Muslim
2.1% Christian (mainly Catholic)
0.19% Evangelical
Status of the church: Anglican and
Methodist churches
Major Religious Sites:
New Banjul Central Mosque

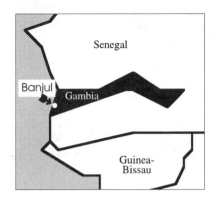

City Significance/History:

Banjul was nothing more than a cluster of mud huts until the need for slave labor arose in more developed countries. The British changed this village into a large trading post.

Alex Haley's book *Roots* traced Kunta Kinte's homeland to Gambia. It was in the village of Juffure where he was captured and taken to the port of Banjul for transport to North America.

Banjul, located at the mouth of the Gambia River, became a destination where slaves were transported. The 700-mile-long river allowed slave traders to capture slaves far inland and transport them easily for auction and deportation in Banjul. Once on the ships, they went to slave plantations throughout the world.

Today Banjul, technically an island, has been connected to the mainland by a bridge. Its location has caused it to be demographically stagnant for years, and this has hurt the economy. However, the mainland suburbs around Banjul have recently experienced rapid growth.

> **"The British left nothing but cricket and the Anglican Church"**
> **–Banjul merchant**

Prayer Points

1. Pray that the church will reach out to the Muslim majority, particularly the Mandingo people of *Roots* fame.

2. Pray that the Anglican and Methodist churches will experience revival.

3. Pray for the ministries working with the young people who have moved to Banjul seeking work.

4. Pray for continued freedom to proclaim the gospel in this Muslim land.

5. Prison ministry has produced many converts. Pray for more conversions and the reintegration of released prisoners into churches and communities.

6. Pray that the three Sufi brotherhoods would come to base their fellowship in the Holy Spirit.

Bissau
(bi-**soh**)

Day 2

Meaning: "it's finished"
Country: Guinea–Bissau*
Population: 130,000
Poverty: Many poor because
    of socialism
Religious Breakdown:
    48.1%   Traditional Religions
    44.0%   Muslim
    6.7%   Christian (mainly Catholic)
    0.84% Evangelical
Status of the church: 36 national pastors
    in the country, a maturing church
Major Religious Sites: Avenue de Cintura
    Mosque, Roman Catholic Cathedral,
    Curadores Healing Houses (Animist)

City Significance/History:

Years ago, Muslim semi-nomadic herdsmen moved east into the flat lands and settled in Bissau. It became the capital of Portuguese Guinea, an overseas colony of Portugal. The Portuguese set up a fortified post here in 1765 to administrate their interests in the area.

Today it is the center for commerce and industry, with exports of rice and coconut products. It is the largest city and capital of Guinea-Bissau.

Before Islam or Christianity entered the area, many of the African people lived in fear of, yet worshiped, different spirits and fetishes (a practice called animism, spiritism, or traditional religion). These ancient beliefs mixed with whatever religion was laid over the top of them.

> **These ancient beliefs mix with whatever religion is laid over the top of them**

Therefore, strange animistic practices can be seen in people who are Muslim or Christians. The spiritual bondage which the people experience is common among those who practice spiritism. Many people wear amulets and put symbols on their homes to avoid getting the "evil eye," a much-feared curse that can even kill a child.

Prayer Points

1. Pray that past animistic practices will be renounced by the believers, replacing them with deep trust and faith in the power of Jesus.

2. Pray for the Christians to have confidence in witnessing to Muslims.

3. Pray for financial blessing on the believers, whose poverty makes it difficult to support their pastors, and for more workers and national pastors to be raised up. Pray for outreach to the new, large townships being built on the outskirts of the city.

4. Pray against the growth and influence of new religious groups such as the Jehovah's Witnesses, Bahais, Moonies, and New Apostolics.

5. Many young people have migrated from the interior seeking education and employment. Pray that they will find the gospel instead of materialism, disillusionment, and, increasingly, atheism.

Conakry
(kon-uh-kree)

Day 2

Meaning: unknown
Country: Guinea*
Population: 1,734,000
Poverty: Much poverty because of government corruption
Religious Breakdown:
- 94.0% Muslim
- 2.0% Traditional Religions
- 4.0% Christian
- 0.04% Evangelical

Status of the church: Roman Catholic— 4, Anglican—1, Christian and Missionary Alliance—1
Major Religious Sites:
Grand Mosque

City Significance/History:

Conakry began as a small fishing village on Tomba Island and has since developed into the country's main port, educational center, and capital.

After independence from France in 1958, Guinea embraced Marxist ideology. Christians suffered greatly under the Marxist pro-Islamic government. The city went into decline, with the infrastructure almost completely collapsing. The streets became extremely dirty, with garbage everywhere.

A military coup in 1984 overthrew the Marxist regime and restored basic freedoms. The military government has been struggling to bring recovery and economic progress since entering power. The city's appearance has not improved —changes come slowly. Presently there is religious liberty for Christian witness and missionary activity.

During the rainy season, Conakry may receive as much as 12 feet of rain. Iron and bauxite mining has permitted the city to grow slowly in recent years.

> **Conakry is struggling to bring economic recovery**

Prayer Points

1. Pray for the economic recovery of the city—that jobs would be created and that the current government would be wise in the implementation of reforms.

2. Pray that freedom for Christian witness and missionary activity would continue.

3. Pray for the Christians to have a vision for evangelizing the Muslim majority.

4. Pray for the gospel to become established among the three dominant Muslim peoples — the Maninka, the Fula, and the Susu.

5. Many new missions agencies have come since 1985. Pray for unity and cooperation among these as well as with the national churches.

Bamako
(bam-uh-koh)

Meaning: "crocodile pool"
Country: Mali*
Population: 680,000
Poverty: Drought and famine have
  caused an increase in poverty
Religious Breakdown:
  86.3%   Muslim
  9.2%   Traditional Religions
  3.7%   Christian
  0.7%   Evangelical
Status of the church:
  30 small churches
Major Religious Sites:
  Great Mosque, Hamdallaye Islamic
  Center, Sorcery and Fetish Bazaar

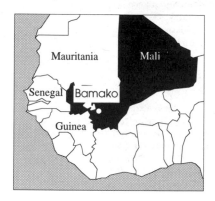

City Significance/History:

Five hundred years ago Bamako was a Muslim trading center in the ancient Mali empire. When the French arrived in 1880, this metropolis had dwindled to approximately 1000 people. Situated on the fertile Niger River, the city again has a growing population.

Musa and his 13-year-old younger brother, Mamadou, live in a small farming village some 300 kilometers from Bamako. This year they will find a ride on a truck going to the big city. This will cost money, but the amount they will receive for their fruits and vegetables will be at least double in the city. Musa tells his brother that last year he was able to

sell the majority of what they had grown. He had learned from a Brazilian Christian man about new seeds that produce a greater harvest. He bought only a few because they were expensive. This year he will buy more. The man's words about these seeds were true and worth the extra money.

This annual migration of about 100,000 people takes place for many young farmers as they leave their villages with goods grown during the rainy season, and seek to sell them during the dry season. Many would like to stay in the city, but cannot because jobs are very hard to find.

Prayer Points

1. Pray for more workers to evangelize the city and start outreaches in the suburbs.

2. Pray that Radio Bamako will expand its audience, that Christian programming on national TV will bear fruit, and that the literature ministry will flourish.

3. Pray that the Bambara people around Bamako may be evangelized and discipled.

4. Pray that the Hamdallye imam (religious leader) would no longer resist Christian activities, particularly public crusades, and stop calling for an Islamic state.

5. Koulouba Hill overlooking the city is noted both as a hiding place for thieves and as the site of the presidential palace. Pray that corruption and thievery, which is undermining the nation, would cease and that all who are leading from atop this hill would be overcome by the gospel of Christ.

Ouagadougou
(wah-guh-**doo**-goo)

Day 3

Meaning: "place of the Ouaga people"
Country: Burkina Faso*
Population: 437,000
Poverty: Much malnutrition, especially among children
Religious Breakdown:
48.0% Muslim
33.0% Traditional Religions
19.0% Christian (mainly Catholic)
4.3% Evangelical
Status of the church: 100% increase in the last 15 years
Major Religious Sites:
Grand Mosque

City Significance/History:

Historically, the city was the capital of the Mossi Kingdom. Since the rule of Naba Dulugu in the late 18th century, it has been predominantly Muslim. At nearby Crocodile Lake homage is paid to the crocodile.

Mossi carries his sick son as he walks to the market. Skillets and pots hang on the walls of the corner store. Turning left he sees the religious man selling portions of scripture from the Koran. The man offers him one in a gazelle skin pouch. Reasoning to himself, "Allah is great, but I need medicine today," he moves on.

Laughter fills the market, but fear grips Mossi's heart. His son has been sick for two weeks and no one knows what to do. Just past the religious man, Mossi looks at a sign with pictures of a drink mixture of water, salt, and sugar. Being illiterate he fails to understand it is a rehydration mix and moves on.

Finally, he reaches the "bush doctors," who squat behind a cloth covered with snakes' heads, dried owls, and lions' tails. A broken antelope's horn pierces a heap of flint off to the left side. With almost his last money, he buys a little square of elephant hide as the prescription given by the bush doctor. Three days later his son dies of dehydration caused by diarrhea.

Prayer Points

1. Pray that the power of idolatry, fetishism, and secret societies will be broken in Jesus' name.

2. Pray for a greater ministry to students, particularly to those at Ouagadougou University.

3. Pray that the church can be a healing agent in the midst of social upheavals and family breakdowns caused by urban migration.

4. Because of the high illiteracy rate, the need for audio scripture is great. Scripture portions are available in six languages, but not in audio form. Pray for workers and resources to produce these.

5. Pray for continued growth in the church and for leaders to train and disciple the new converts.

Algiers
(al-**jeerz**)

Day 3

Meaning: "the islands"
Country: Algeria*
Population: 3,722,000
Poverty: No major slums, much unemployment
Religious Breakdown:
   99.4%   Muslim
   0.4%   Christian
   0.07% Evangelical
Status of the church:
   2 small fellowships
Major Religious Sites: Djemaa el Jedid
   (Fishermen or New) Mosque, Djemaa el
   Kebir (Great) Mosque, Sidi
   Abderrahaman Mosque

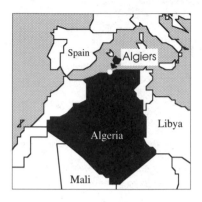

City Significance/History:

Algiers was an important commercial outpost first under Phoenicia and later under Carthage, Rome, and Byzantium. Pirates used this area as a protected location, and the Barbary coast began to get a reputation in the 16th century. The Ottoman Empire, based in Turkey, conquered much of North Africa. The Ottoman set up beys—provincial governors—over its territories—and one was based in Algiers. The French controlled the area for the next 130 years, leading up to Algeria's independence in 1962.

In recent years, the Islamic fundamentalists have gained more and more political power. The political leaders are having an increasingly hard time protecting the rights of women.

> **Islamic fundamentalists have gained more political power**

In the last few years, the Islamic religious men have tried to force the Muslim women to wear the veil. The veil not only covers the face of the women, but represents a society where women are little more than possessions owned by their husbands. If Islamic law is placed on the women, what freedom these women have today will be removed from them.

Prayer Points

1. Pray for the Muslim women as more Islamic laws are placed on them. These laws will restrict their freedom and make them second-class citizens. Pray for Christian marriages and godly families to be raised up.

2. Pray for the foreign population. In the last few years the Islamic fundamentalists have been targeting the foreigners with violent acts, and many have been killed. Missionaries have been affected and many forced to leave.

3. Pray for a peaceful solution to the severe political bloodshed initiated by the Islamists in what has been called "The Second Algerian War." Fundamentalists are seeking to install a government similar to the Iranian Islamic state.

4. Pray for the security of Berber and Arab Christians and the underground churches. Some have received death threats, and murders occur regularly in the city.

Tunis
(too-nis)

Meaning: uncertain
Country: Tunisia*
Population: 1,935,000
Poverty: No major slums,
　much unemployment
Religious Breakdown:
　99.49%　Muslim
　0.25%　Jewish
　0.25%　Christian
　0.01%　Evangelical
Status of the church: A few Tunisian
　evangelicals, some Roman Catholics
Major Religious Sites:
　Zitouna Mosque and Islamic University,
　Rue Jemaa es Zituna Mosque

City Significance/History:

Tunis originally sprang up as a Phoenician trading post nearly 3000 years ago. The ancient Carthaginian Empire was centered in Carthage—now an archaeological site outside Tunis. Child sacrifice was practiced by the people to worship Baal. Among the ruins a graveyard for children and an altar where children were sacrificed have been unearthed. On the Bougarneen mountain outside of Tunis it is reported that child sacrifice still takes place.

After Carthage was destroyed by the Romans in 146 BC, Tunis grew as a Roman, Byzantine, and finally an Arab city. In 1962 French rule ended.

The government of Tunisia has been fighting to keep the country out of the hands of the Islamic fundamentalist group Ennahdha. They have even placed some of its more radical members in prison, charging them with treason. Unemployment and a sluggish economy have not helped the government, but they are seeking to enhance trade with industrialized nations.

Tunis has been the headquarters for the Arab league and the Palestine Liberation Organization (PLO). It was Yasir Arafat's home and where the PLO gave leadership to the Palestinians when the group was outlawed in Israel.

═══ Prayer Points ═══

1. Pray against the spirit of materialism which strongly grips the people's hearts. Individually and nationally the highest priority is peace and prosperity.

2. Lift before the Lord the child sacrifice situation—asking him to remove whatever spiritual strongholds might still remain.

3. Pray that God would use economic hardships to draw Tunisians to himself.

4. Pray for unity in the small Christian community and against complacency, for life is comfortable.

5. Pray that God would reveal his holiness to the Tunisians so that they will be convicted of sin—Tunis has one of the lowest percentages of Christians.

6. Pray that the government would ease its strict controls, allowing individuals freedom to investigate the gospel.

Tripoli
(**trip**-uh-lee)

Day 3

Meaning: a natural abrasive
Country: Libya*
Population: 1,828,000
Poverty: Oil has increased the
   standard of living
Religious Breakdown:
  96.0%   Muslim
   3.0%   Christian
   0.08% Evangelical
Status of the church:
   A handful of Libyan believers
Major Religious Sites:
   Gurgi Mosque, Karamanli Mosque

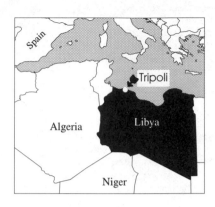

City Significance/History:

Also called Tarabulus, Tripoli is a seaport first settled by the Phoenicians. One of the first items exported was tripoli, a light-colored, very fine powder used as an abrasive or for polishing. Desert traders also brought gold, ivory, ebony, dates, and other goods by camel caravans to Tripoli.

History has proven to be very violent for the city and people of Tripoli, with one conqueror after another fighting for this city. The Phoenician rule was replaced by the Romans, then Vandals, Byzantines, Arabs (who brought Islam to the area), Spanish, Turks (as a colonial capital for the Ottoman Empire), Italians, and British before Libya became an independent kingdom in 1951.

On September 1, 1969, modern-day Libya was established through a coup that placed Muammar Qadhafi in power. He balances the government between Islamic fundamentalists who desire a stronger Islamic state, and rivalries within the regime itself.

Tripoli is the capital city of Qadhafi's military regime. Libya is known as a strong force behind the spread of Islam in other nations and for international terrorist activities. It is also the headquarters for the Islamic Call, a major Islamic mission organization.

Prayer Points

1. Pray that the terrorist activity emanating from here would stop and that the financial support of terrorism would end.

2. Pray that evangelism would again be allowed in Libya.

3. Pray that radio programming beamed into the city would find a responsive audience and many would turn to the Lord.

4. Pray that foreign Christians working in Tripoli would have wisdom, boldness, and protection as they witness to Libyans. Many of these workers can only share their faith with people they trust, who will not turn them into the police.

5. Pray that God would thwart the evangelistic plans of the Islamic Call and bring many to himself who would otherwise be missionaries for Islam.

Cotonou
(koh-teh-noo)

Meaning: unknown
Country: Benin*
Population: 501,000
Poverty: Growing economic opportunities
with the fall of communism
Religious Breakdown:
  50.0%   Animist
  20.0%   Muslim
  28.2%   Christian (mainly Catholic)
  1.96%   Evangelical
Status of the church: (including Porto Novo)
  17 evangelical with 4000 members, 60,000
  African Independent Church members
Major Religious Sites:
  Central Mosque

City Significance/History:

Although neighboring Porto Novo is the official capital, most government and diplomatic functions occur in Cotonou. In 1960 Benin received its independence from France. In 1991 democracy replaced the Marxist government that had ruled for over a decade. The cult of voodoo was born in Benin, and it is but one expression of animistic religion keeping people in spiritual bondage.

The countries just south of the Sahara Desert were the nearest place for developing nations to receive cheap slave labor. Thus port cities grew, slave ships came and went, and African families were torn to pieces.

Cotonou was one of the centers for the deportation of slaves. The coast in this area became known as the "Slave Coast."

For those countries responsible for the sin against these African people, this is a day to repent and ask for forgiveness.

For those of African heritage, whose ancestors were victims of the slave trade, give the blessing of forgiveness, just as Christ has forgiven.

On this day, millions of people will be praying prayers of repentance and millions will be giving forgiveness. May Christ be glorified!

Prayer Points

1. For those countries who received African slave labor, pray prayers of repentance for the acts of your fathers. Ask God to wipe away any sin that remains.

2. For those families who were victims of the slave trade, give the blessing of forgiveness to the children of those who enslaved your forefathers.

3. God is more powerful than all traditional religions and voodoo practices. Pray that God would reveal his mighty power in Cotonou, and break the hold of animism.

4. Pray for workers to reach the unevangelized Muslims who comprise 20% of the urban population.

5. Pray for continued growth in the church and for leaders to be trained as pastors.

Niamey
(nee-uh-may)

Meaning: unknown
Country: Niger*
Population: 430,000
Poverty: Slum communities, strained resources because of rural migration
Religious Breakdown:
  90.5% Muslim
   9.0% Traditional Religions
   0.38% Christian
   0.1% Evangelical
Status of the church: The number of evangelicals have doubled since 1980
Major Religious Sites:
  New Grand Mosque,
  Old Grand Mosque

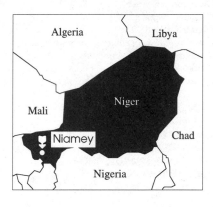

City Significance/History:

Niamey began as an agricultural village where three different ethnic groups—the Maouri, Zerma, and Fulani—formed a village on the banks of the Niger River.

At the turn of the century, Niamey became a small French military outpost to help navigators on the river and to control the inland interests of France. Its river location allowed for travel into many of the surrounding countries. For many people in West Africa, the Niger River is a source of life and income.

In 1930 the city had about 2000 people. This little village on the river has grown to over 400,000 people today. It is Niger's capital and largest city. Drought has forced many people to move to Niamey from rural areas and other neighboring countries. These people have brought an international flavor with them and turned Niamey into a trading center.

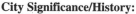

> **"As the river is eternal, so will my work be eternal"**
> **—Niger proverb**

Prayer Points

1. Pray for workers to evangelize this Muslim city that is open to the gospel.

2. Pray that God would supernaturally reveal himself to students at the Islamic University near Niamey.

3. Emigration and migration has forced rapid growth in the city. Pray that the needs of the poor would be met and that Jesus would be known.

4. Pray that young Christians would be able to find work and not be pressured to abandon their faith in exchange for job security—that their faith would grow strong.

5. Pray that God would raise up more Christian leaders from the local population.

6. Many are attracted to Christianity, but fear possible persecution. Pray for a lessening of persecution, strength to believe, and boldness to live for Christ.

Kano
(kahn-oh)

Meaning: unknown
Country: Nigeria, Kano State*
Population: 660,000
Poverty: Many live in mud block homes
  with poor nutrition, sanitation, and health
Religious Breakdown:
  80.0%   Muslim
   5.0%   Traditional Religion
  14.9%   Christian
   0.1%   Evangelical
Status of the church: None in the old
  walled city, Hausa people are converting
Major Religious Sites: Central Mosque,
  New Mosque

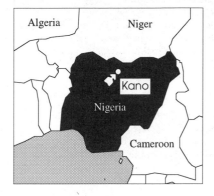

City Significance/History:

In the middle of Nigeria there is an imaginary line drawn. The forces behind it have spiritual roots. To the north of this line, the knowledge of Christ is almost nil. From the line south, amazing church growth has occurred. The capital, the largest city, and most churches are in Nigeria's south.

Kano, Nigeria's third largest city, is the oldest city in West Africa. It has been a commercial center in the region for hundreds of years. Camel caravans have been replaced by trucks, but it is still a lively city.

Some miles away from Kano, the tall, white minarets and green tile dome of the mosque tower appear above the heat waves lifting off the desert sand. The interior part of the city is surrounded by a wall. Inside this wall on Friday, the holy day, 50,000 Muslims will bathe, remove their shoes, and enter the mosque to pray.

As the mosque gets closer, this ancient Hausa city takes on shape. A few shade trees cover one-story adobe homes. The walls are thick to give warmth in the winter, and bring needy relief from the sun during the summer. Streets run in all directions, twisting and turning as the city continues to grow, as homes are being built out of the earth around them.

Prayer Points

1. Pray that Christian ministries may be established in Greater Kano, the Muslim city center which is separated by a physical wall. Pray that the spiritual wall, which it symbolizes, may be broken down in the hearts of the Kanawas.

2. Pray that the city's high divorce rate may be lowered. This is caused by forced marriages of girls aged 10-12, who become pregnant and damage their reproductive organs at delivery. Husbands then divorce their sterile wives.

3. Pray that the burning of churches and persecution of Christian leaders stop—that civic officials will allow outdoor crusades for evangelism.

4. Pray that Christian professionals would develop effective cross-cultural evangelistic strategies such as medical service and well drilling.

5. Pray for missionaries to be raised up among the Issawa, Maguzawa, and Bade tribes.

N'Djamena
(en-**jah**-muh-nuh)

Day 4

Meaning: "we rested"
Country: Chad*
Population: 729,000
Poverty: Many living near death
Religious Breakdown:
   51.0% Muslim
   35.1% Christian
   13.3% Evangelical
Status of the church: 40 churches, fear
  of persecution
Major Religious Sites:
  Grand Mosque,
  King Faisal Mosque and School

City Significance/History:

Lake Chad—once the 11th largest lake in the world—has been shrinking in the last 100 years due to the growth of the Sahara. The receding water leaves about three inches of topsoil behind on the open land. Few nomadic people understand how to harvest crops, or have the resources to buy seeds or seedlings.

For people like the Muslim Tuaregs, growing vegetables on one small section of land does not satisfy their nomadic nature. The vast lands of Chad are their dwelling, not the capital city. But famines have forced cultural changes.

In the last twenty years, N'Djamena has experienced rapid growth due to the famine and the hope of a better life in the big city. However, even the city has felt the effects of economic decline.

The government created feeding centers on the routes people were taking to the capital in order to control the growth of the city. These centers have become cities in themselves. Cotton was one of the main exports of the country; however, famine and the market collapse have since changed that income.

Today Chad is one of the poorest countries in the world. The drought has ended, but living conditions have remained precarious.

Prayer Points

1. Pray for the training of pastors and evangelists at the Shalom Higher School of Theology—that the believers' fear of witnessing to Muslims would disappear.

2. Pray that the city will cease being a center for propagating Islam and instead be a center for propagating the gospel.

3. Pray for the poor living around N'Djamena. Many people do not have enough food.

4. Pray that those coming to N'Djamena for work would be receptive to the gospel— that Christians who must live with Muslim relatives would not convert to Islam.

5. Pray that the suspicion and animosity among the hundred plus ethnic groups would find unity in the reconciling power of Jesus Christ.

6. Pray for the development of the New Testament and more Christian literature in the Chad Arabic dialect.

Khartoum
(kahr-**toom**)

Meaning: "elephant's trunk"
Country: Sudan*
Population: 2,477,000
Poverty: 2.8 million displaced people
not officially counted in Sudan's population
Religious Breakdown:
70.0%   Muslim
11.0%   Traditional Religions
16.0%   Christian
3.1%   Evangelical
Status of the church: Growth among
relocated southerners, a few Muslim converts
Major Religious Sites: Hamed al Niel Mosque,
El Kabir Mosque, Mahadi's Tomb

City Significance/History:

The spread of Christianity in the early centuries followed trade routes. It remained north of the Sahara Desert and along the Mediterranean Sea, but was able to penetrate into Sudan because of the Nile River.

The White and Blue Nile rivers joined together to make a fertile agricultural zone where life was pleasant and crops grew well. Established nearby was Soba, the capital of the Christian kingdom of Nubia (c. 580), not far from present-day Khartoum. By the 14th century, an active Christian kingdom was almost extinct as Islam grew. During the 19th century Khartoum became an export location for slaves and ivory.

The silver-domed mosque and minarets mark this Islamic capital. Islam has been growing in the north of Sudan as Muslim holy men lead the country into *sharia* (Islamic) law. This law is forced on the Muslims and non-Muslims alike.

The famine in the south has caused death and hardship on the non-Muslim peoples. People do seek help in Khartoum but are banished to the harsh southern desert—1 1/2 million have died and over 5 million are internal refugees. Aid sent to Sudan rarely reaches the needy. The suffering has heightened as the government has stymied relief efforts.

Prayer Points

1. Pray for peace and that relief shipments can get to the people. Pray that Christian relief agencies can get in and be protected from hostile political forces.

2. Pray that workers can train and teach local leaders. Pray that Sudanese Christians will then evangelize and disciple new believers to carry on the gospel, thus helping new churches to grow.

3. Pray for Bible translation work to continue and for more translators; pray also for workers in literacy training.

4. Pray that Muslims and non-Muslims would see the way the Muslim government is treating non-Muslims and this would cause them to turn to Christ.

5. Pray for financial resources to rebuild the church and for strength to withstand suffering.

Djibouti

(jee-**boo**-tee)

Meaning: "queen of the sands"
Country: Djibouti*
Population: 137,000
Poverty: 85% unemployment
Religious Breakdown:
   94.6% Muslim
   4.6%   Christian (mainly Catholic)
   0.07% Evangelical
Status of the church: A few small
   fellowships
Major Religious Sites:
   Jamac Mosque,
   Altixad Islamic School

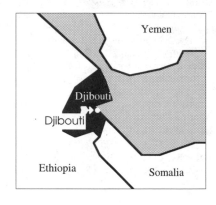

City Significance/History:

Water has dictated the lives of traditionally nomadic shepherds. Two main peoples, the Somalis and Afars, have wandered the desert for centuries seeking water for their herds. At times, wars have started over this valuable resource—water. Under the desert, water can be found, but digging for it is costly.

In a country where 90% of the people are illiterate, Hassan, one of his father's 20 children, is able to take a giant step forward. As a boy he wandered with his nomadic family; however, he has since learned to read, which has set him apart. He managed to go to college and now teaches in Djibouti. It is people like

Hassan who will be the future leaders.

Djibouti, the sole major city, rests on the west side of the strait of Bab el Mandeb, "Gate of Sorrow." This strait separates the Red Sea and the Indian Ocean.

Economically, Djibouti has been hard hit. Unemployment is approximately 85%. One of the main sources of revenue is a 500 mile railroad running from Addis Ababa, the capital of Ethiopia, to Djibouti. To cause even more economic problems, Somalia cut the track. It has now been restored, but the political unrest among all of the countries in the Horn of Africa continues.

Prayer Points

1. With unemployment so high many people are living close to poverty level. Pray for these poor, especially the children who suffer the most.

2. Pray that peace and stability between the Somalis and Afars will continue and that there will be continued openness to a Christian presence.

3. Pray for the missionaries laboring in extreme living conditions, in what is the world's hottest country.

4. Pray for converts to result from ministries involved with education, public health, agriculture, literature, and youth work.

5. Pray for the effective use of literacy programs and the Scriptures in Somali and Afar.

Addis Ababa
(**ad**-is **ab**-uh-buh)

Day 5

Meaning: "new flower"
Country: Ethiopia*
Population: 2,419,000
Poverty: Plastic shantytowns surround the city
Religious Breakdown:
   40.0%   Muslim
   45.0%   Ethiopian Orthodox Church
   5.0%   Traditional Religions
   10.0%   Evangelical
Status of the church: Ancient Orthodox church,
   10 evangelical churches.
Major Religious Sites: Grand Mosque,
   Ethiopian Orthodox Church,
   Menilik Mausoleum

City Significance/History:

The Amharic people of Ethiopia's highlands built their capitol at Addis Ababa, a natural 8000-foot-high fortress. From there, they could control most of the lowlands.

The "King of Kings," Haile Selassie, had reigned almost 50 years as the 225th emperor—claiming descent from the union of the Queen of Sheba and King Solomon of Israel. Ethiopians believe that the ark of the covenant is in Ethiopia. The Christian church started early when the Ethiopian eunuch encountered Philip in Acts 7.

The Ethiopian Marxist revolution of 1974 moved the whole country from the 13th century into the 20th century through 17 years of excessive violence. Drought and political extremism allowed one of the greatest famines in modern history to kill more than a million people. The Derg (communist) political party used extreme fear and coercion to keep people under control. Today this party has been outlawed. Developments have taken place with modern buildings now rising behind the mud-walled huts.

Addis Ababa is the headquarters for both the Organization of African Unity and the United Nations Commission for Africa.

Prayer Points

1. Pray that students in the Bible schools and seminaries would be filled with the Holy Spirit and anointed to preach the gospel powerfully.

2. Pray that the government could lead the country into economic recovery and a higher quality of life for the people.

3. Pray that the poor street children, beggars, and handicapped war veterans would receive food and the gospel.

4. Pray for God to raise up strong family structures that will be a model of a Christian home and marriage.

5. Thousands of high school graduates and other youth cannot find work—pray for the creation of jobs.

Asmara
(as-mar-uh)

Day 5

Meaning: union of 4 city names
Country: Eritrea*
Population: 1,069,000
Poverty: Poverty high, but stabilizing
Religious Breakdown:
  51.0% Muslim
  46.1% Christian
  1.47% Evangelical
Status of the church: Coptics and Evangelicals
  have united because of war
Major Religious Sites:
  Anwar Mosque

City Significance/History:

At the edge of a high plateau rests Asmara, once a beautiful Italian-built city, and now one of the newest capitals in the world. A large university was founded here in 1958.

Ethiopia claimed Eritrea as part of the Ethiopian Empire. Over the last 31 years, Eritrea has sought independence from Ethiopia through violence and political wars. Drought and war led to a famine that killed many.

In 1993, independence was granted and a new country was formed. The beautiful Italian city was marred by machine guns and mortars.

Drought and war led to a famine

Now that rain has started to fall and war is over, reconstruction of the land is beginning. Roads destroyed in the war are being patched, and crops have grown. In the last few years, they have been able to double crop production, allowing for a reduction in foreign aid.

Having fought and died together has allowed the Muslims and Christians to work together towards building a new country. Dropping ethnic differences has also permitted stability and a national identity that in many other countries is falling apart.

Prayer Points

1. Pray for the continued economic recovery of the city and country—that rain would continue to water the crops.

2. Coptic Orthodox and Evangelical Christians have been meeting and even having all night prayer times together. Praise God for this unity that persecution has brought. Pray that revival will enter these churches.

3. Pray for Muslim converts among the Tigre, Afar, Beja, and Saho peoples.

4. Pray for Christian missionaries to return and to serve the church with leadership training, media, and helping ministries.

5. Pray for finances to enable churches to rebuild and repair facilities damaged by fighting.

Mogadishu
(moh-guh-dish-oo)

Meaning: unknown
Country: Somalia*
Population: 849,000
Poverty: Violence and drought have caused great poverty
Religious Breakdown:
   99.9%   Muslim
   0.04%   Christian
   0.03%   Evangelical
Status of the church: Little growth in the last 100 years, a few Somali believers
Major Religious Sites:
   Fakr Al Din Mosque,
   Great Mosque

City Significance/History:

War–drought–devastation, the cycle of life for Saphia. She ran out of food—her two camels and goats died as the ground turned to dust. Eight months pregnant, she decided not to flee with her family to Ethiopia. Instead, she moved to a refugee camp outside Mogadishu, where the streets became battle zones. Daily her husband sought food and work in the city.

Warlords send out war parties against other lords. One day, her husband was standing in a food line. A machine gun mounted on the back of a truck turned the corner and fired on the crowd—he died on the street.

Her baby, now a year old, survives only on what Saphia receives from the food handouts from the refugee workers. She has no choice—she is dependent on the food coming in. She dreams of the days when caring for the camels and goats, and which water hole to go to was the greatest concern. Now her little girl may never see the greatness of Somalia. War seems to be endless. Even if life-giving rain sweeps the land, the bullets will keep life short.

> **Two things are needed— peace and rain**

Prayer Points

1. Pray that the warlords would lose their power and that the government would be stabilized.

2. Pray that the poor would receive the food and care they need.

3. Pray that the streets would be peaceful and safe, not battle zones.

4. Pray that the Christian relief workers can effectively communicate the love of Christ as they distribute food and medicine.

5. Pray for the underground Somali church that is persecuted; many are unmarried men needing Christian wives.

6. Pray for those men to be discipled into faithful and wise leaders in the young church—that they would learn to be warriors for Christ, bringing his peace.

Middle East

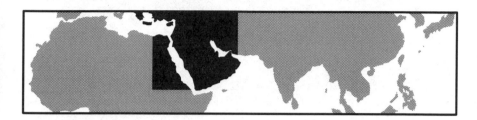

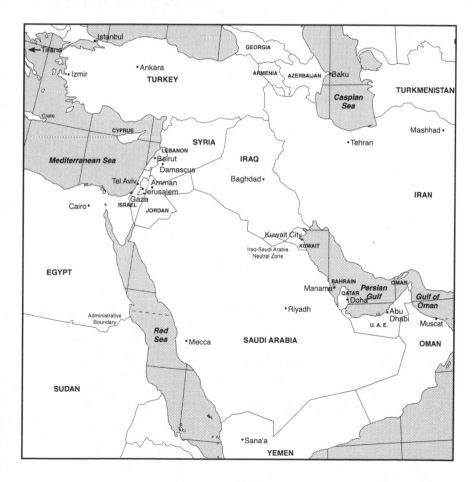

22 Cities

CITY	MAJOR UNREACHED PEOPLES
Mecca	Saudi Arab, Yemeni Arab, Filipino
Riyadh	Saudi Arab, Yemeni Arab, Pakistani
Sana'a	North Yemeni Arab, South Yemeni Arab, Somali
Muscat	Omani Arab, Balochi, Mahra
Abu Dhabi	Arab, Bedouin Arab, Irani Arab
Doha	Qatari Arab, Urdu, Baloch, Lebanese
Manama	Bahraini Arab, Palestinian Arab, Kurd, Malayali
Kuwait City	Arab, Kurd, Numerous Expatriates
Beirut	Lebanese, Palestinian Arab, Druze, Kurd
Tirana	Tosk, Gypsy, Vlash
Cairo	Bedouin, Arabized Berber, Egyptian Arab, Halebi Gypsy
Amman	Palestinian Arab, Jordanian Arab, Bedouin, Adygcy
Damascus	Bedouin Arab, Western Kurd, Turkmen, Palestinian Arab
Gaza	Palestinian Arab, Jew
Jerusalem	Arab, Jew, Bedouin
Tel Aviv	Jew, Palestinian Arab, Bedouin, Farsi
Istanbul	Turk, Persian, Levantine Arab, Turkish Kurd
Ankara	Turk, Persian, Turkish Kurd, Crimean Tatar
Izmir	Turk, Turkish Kurd, Persian
Baghdad	Iraqi Arab, Iraqi Kurd, Turkmen
Tehran	Luri, Mazanderani, Persian, Qashqai
Mashhad	Hazaras, Luri, Persian, Turkmen

Mecca
(mek-uh)

Day 6

Meaning: "the revered"
Country: Saudi Arabia
Population: 884,000
Poverty: Rare among Saudis,
prevalent among 3rd World expatriates
Religious Breakdown:
100% Muslim, the public or private
practice of any religion other than
Islam is totally prohibited
Status of the church: None known, maybe an
underground remnant
Major Religious Sites: Grand Mosque,
Ka'aba Shrine, Well of Zam Zam (said to be
the well provided by God for Hagar and
Ishmael)

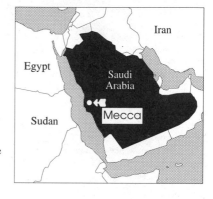

City Significance/History:

Mecca is the focal point of Islam. One-fifth of the world's population looks to this city as their most holy site. Devout Muslims pray facing Mecca five times a day, for mosques all over the world are constructed with their front wall facing Mecca.

In 571, Muhammad was born in the city. Disillusioned with the pagan worship of many gods, Muhammad started to preach there is only one God—Allah, the moon god. After traveling around most of Arabia, he returned to Mecca shortly before he died.

At the center of the Grand Mosque's courtyard rests the Ka'aba, the black stone. Islamic tradition says the Ka'aba, a replica of God's heavenly home, was built by Abraham and Ishmael. (Muslims trace their lineage back to Abraham through Ishmael.) The Ka'aba housed some 360 gods, one of which was Allah.

The Koran (Islam's holy book) states that every Muslim must make a pilgrimage (*Hajj*) to Mecca at least once in his life. On the ninth day of the month of Zhul Hijjah according to the Muslim lunar calendar, millions of pilgrims pray on top of Mount Arafat just outside Mecca. This is the world's largest religious gathering. It is unlawful for any Christian to enter this holy Muslim city.

Prayer Points

1. Pray that the Ka'aba and the mystical powers behind it would be bound from captivating millions of Islamic souls.

2. Pray that the Muslims performing the annual *Hajj* would be disappointed with the commercialism of the city and that those seeking God would find Jesus.

3. Pray that the Islamic religious leaders and religious police would have miraculous encounters like Paul on the road to Damascus. Without God working supernaturally the city will not directly hear the gospel, except through radio.

4. Pray that King Fahd and the royal family would allow Christians to work, reside, and worship openly in Mecca. Pray for strength for existing believers.

5. Pray for the neighboring city of Medina, Islam's 2nd holiest city.

Riyadh
(ree-**yahd**)

Meaning: "orchard" or "garden"
Country: Saudi Arabia*
Population: 2,664,000
Poverty: Rare among Saudis,
　prevalent with 3ʳᵈ World expatriates
Religious Breakdown:
　90.0% Muslim
　4.0% Hindu (expatriates)
　5.0% Christian (expatriates)
　1.0% Evangelical
Status of the church: A few underground
　believers
Major Religious Sites: Imam University,
　King Faisal Islamic Center, over 2000
　mosques of different sizes

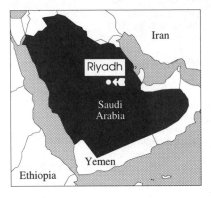

City Significance/History:

Tradition tells of the apostle Bartholomew wandering around Arabia with the message of the Savior. By the 6ᵗʰ century, Christianity was firmly established; however, 100 years later it was completely replaced by Islam, now the official Saudi religion.

A few oases marked the location of a small settlement at the heart of the dry rocky plateau. The coastal areas allowed for travel and trade, but few people ventured through Riyadh.

In 1902, Abdul Aziz recaptured the city from the Ottomans and forever changed its destiny. He designed it to be the national capital, but it still remained isolated and a mud-walled city of a few

clay palaces. Jiddah, on the Red Sea, grew but Riyadh saw little change.

Oil brought more wealth—Riyadh started towards modernization in the 1950s. Because of the recent development, it is the most modern capital in the world. Sand and mud walls have given way to marble palaces, mosques, and schools, such as Imam University, a world center of Islamic theology and outreach.

The revenue from oil allowed for this explosion of growth. Even the poor Saudis have benefited from oil. They have moved out of the slum communities into housing provided by the government.

Prayer Points

1. Pray that King Fahd and the royal family would be moved by God to allow Christian worship—this is an important step towards more people hearing of Jesus.

2. Pray that God would continue to shake and transform the Saudi finances (now in deficit). If revenues remain low, then they would have to stop funding the worldwide expansion of Islam. Pray for tentmakers to be called to Riyadh.

3. Pray that the *Wahabbi* religious leader and the *Mutawwa'in* religious police, who are persecuting the church, would encounter the Lord Jesus.

4. Pray that God could break the stranglehold of Islam in educational institutions, which requires that 70% of all education be devoted to the study of Islam.

5. Pray for the underground church to grow strong and remain vibrant in the midst of persecution—that they could endure with great joy.

Sana'a
(sah-**nah**)

Meaning: "fortified place"
Country: Yemen*
Population: 503,600
Poverty: Poorest Arabian country
Religious Breakdown:
  99.9%   Muslim
  0.06% Christian
  0.02% Evangelical
Status of the church:
  A few secret Yemeni believers
Major Religious Sites:
  Great Mosque, Al-Jami Al-Kabir Mosque,
  Salah ad-Din Mosque, al-Mutwakil Mosque,
  Muslim Brotherhood Headquarters

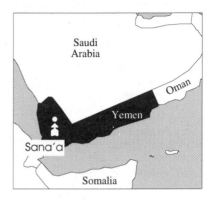

City Significance/History:

The original name of the capital city of Yemen is "Medinat Som," translated the "city of Shem." Tradition holds that after the Flood, Shem, the son of Noah, built this city on the volcanic plain 2,225 meters above sea level.

By the turn of the 1ˢᵗ century, it had become a fortified city (still one of the largest and best preserved cities in the Arab world) along the great incense road leading to the Mediterranean. Myrrh and frankincense grew naturally becoming valuable trade items.

South Yemen was formed in 1967, and became the world's only Arab Marxist state. It signed a 20-year friendship treaty with the USSR, which allowed Soviet troops in Yemen. North Yemen looked to the West politically.

The fall of communism in the world enabled Yemen to unite and Sana'a to become the capital, although sporadic fighting continues. Economic reforms have caused tension. The government is trying to bring economic growth to the poorest of the Arabian Peninsula countries. Riots have broken out in Sana'a due to the continued devaluing of the currency (annual inflation has run 100% in recent years) and Islamic religious differences from north (Shi'ite) to south (Sunni).

═══ Prayer Points ═══

1. The Muslim Brotherhood is very anti-Christian and is trying to stop all Christian activity. Pray that their efforts are unsuccessful.

2. Most residents have never heard the gospel because the city was sealed for over 1,300 years. Pray for fruit from Christian radio programs and boldness for the relief workers involved in health and educational projects.

3. Pray for strength for the believers who are under intense pressure from relatives and civil authorities to renounce their faith.

4. Pray that peace and reconciliation may prevail between the northern and southern factions in the recent civil war. Pray that reforms will bring economic relief.

5. Pray against the spirit of fear that is especially intense here because of the way the Imam has exercised his authority.

Muscat

(mus-**kat**)

Meaning: "place of falling" or "anchorage"
Country: Oman*
Population: 177,000
Poverty: Oil has brought economic growth
Religious Breakdown:

   95.5%   Muslim
   1.6%   Hindu
   2.5%   Christian
   0.16%   Evangelical

Status of the church: Two very small
   fellowships in the country
Major Religious Sites:
   Khor Mosque,
   Ali Musa Mosque

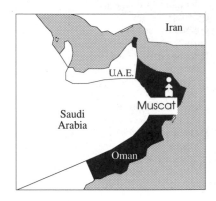

City Significance/History:

Muscat has been a strategic seaport city for the last one thousand years. A mud fort, dwarfed by the volcanic mountains overhead, provided protection for the capital city. The local people would fish, mine lime, or grow dates as their main income, but the sea was their connection to the outside world.

Sinbad, the famous sailor, sailed from Muscat to exotic places like India and China. He would trade lime, dates, and other goods from the Middle East for rice, coffee, and tea. Other ships would stop here before heading into the Persian Gulf or down the east side of Africa. Because of its location, the Portuguese captured Muscat and set up a regional stronghold in the 1580s. They were later replaced by the Al-Busaid Dynasty, who ruled as far as East Africa. By the mid-17th century, Muscat was back in the hands of the Omani. In 1890 Samuel Zwemer established a medical mission work, which still continues.

Oil found in the desert has brought Muscat into the 20st century. After a palace coup, Sultan Qaboos Bin Said replaced his father as the ruler. The city has grown to include two adjacent cities—Mutrah and Ruwi. Muscat is once again a booming area where oil tankers have replaced the trading ships of old.

Prayer Points

1. Pray for strength and boldness for the few indigenous believers, and that churches can be planted.

2. Pray that the sultan would allow Omani citizens freedom of religion.

3. Pray that radio broadcasts and literature distribution would reach the Muslim majority.

4. Pray that expatriate believers working in the city would show a Christian witness through their lifestyle.

5. Pray that ongoing medical missions work would show Christ's love to the people.

Abu Dhabi
(ah-boo dah-bee)

Meaning: unknown
Country: United Arab Emirates*
Population: 730,000
Poverty: In 20 years oil has turned
   poverty to fabulous wealth
Religious Breakdown:
   84.6%   Muslim
   4.7%   Hindu
   8.7%   Christian (among expatriates)
   0.33%   Evangelical
Status of the church: Expatriates have churches,
   only a few Arab believers
Major Religious Sites:
   New Bazaar Mosque

City Significance/History:

Originating from a sandy swamp, the whitewashed fort, Al-Husn Palace, of Abu Dhabi comes into view. A little over 200 years ago, an ancestor of the present shaikh's family moved from the desert to the island, and built a fort around the sweet water spring. Date farming and fishing provided the fort with food. Pearls opened the door for trade and export with India and Europe.

25 years ago the city looked little different than in ancient days. It was the capital of the seven United Arab Emirates. (Abu Dhabi is also the name of the largest and richest of these emirates, which comprises over 90% of the emirates' total area.) But the growth and riches of oil were just starting to be felt. Today, caught between the sand dunes of Arabia and the waves of the Persian Gulf, a modern city has grown fast. Early construction on the sand bars proved disastrous for building with multi-stories. Many sank and had to be destroyed. That problem corrected, a glass and concrete city now rises above the sand.

80% of the people living in Abu Dhabi are expatriates, coming from poorer Gulf states and places like India or Pakistan. Many of these expatriates work in servant roles, roles that the U.A.E. Arabs do not desire to do.

Prayer Points

1. Pray that the Supreme Council would allow freedom of religion for the citizens.

2. Pray that expatriate believers would have the opportunity to share the gospel with their Arab coworkers.

3. Pray for the establishment of an indigenous Arab church and that leaders would be raised up.

4. Pray that the people would see Christ's love demonstrated by the Christian medical agencies serving here.

5. Pray that videos, radio broadcasts, and literature would bear fruit in evangelizing all people groups.

Doha
(doh-hah)

Meaning: "half-circle"
Country: Qatar*
Population: 340,000
Poverty: Great wealth, Asian workers live
    in poverty
Religious Breakdown:
   91.4%   Muslim
   2.0%   Hindu
   6.0%   Christian (among expatriates)
   0.53% Evangelical
Status of the church: No Qatari
   believers before 1985
Major Religious Sites:
   Grand Mosque

City Significance/History:

The expanding desert proved a hard place to live. Bedouins would move from one oasis to another trying to make a living by trading dates and other goods. The coastal areas of the Persian Gulf allowed for a little more stability, providing food through fishing and a little income by diving for pearls. Doha was settled as these nomadic Bedouins chose to fish instead of wander the desert.

This small city remained poor and of little interest to the outside world for most of its history. Bahrain and Qatar have fought for the rights to the rich pearl beds, but otherwise, little importance was given to Doha, the country's capital. The British, a protector of Qatar until its independence in 1971, did not even have a representative in the country until after oil was found.

Just before World War II, Qatar was found to be oil rich. Ten years passed until oil production began. The whole country started to prosper because of the wealth of the black gold. The country also has some of the world's largest gas reserves. The pearl beds have dried up, but now oil rights have been the center of political squabbles between Bahrain and Qatar.

> **Qatar was found to be oil rich**

Prayer Points

1. Pray that some nonresident Qatari believers may return home and become the core of an indigenous church.

2. Pray that the emir would lift legal prohibitions against evangelizing Muslims.

3. Pray that the expatriate Christians working in Doha may be fruitful in their friendship evangelism.

4. Pray that evangelism utilizing radio and video might touch many lives.

5. Pray that the materialistic lifestyle produced by the great oil wealth would bring disillusionment and a renewed search for spiritual truth in Jesus.

6. Pray that students at Qatar University might be reached with the gospel.

Manama
(ma-**na**-muh)

Meaning: "place of rest"
Country: Bahrain*
Population: 270,000
Poverty: Great wealth
Religious Breakdown:
- 85.0%   Muslim
- 6.2%   Hindu
- 7.2%   Christian (among expatriates)
- 0.77% Evangelical

Status of the church: Expatriates can worship freely, a few national believers
Major Religious Sites: Juma (Friday) Mosque, Beit al-Quaran Islamic Center, Al Fateh Islamic Center

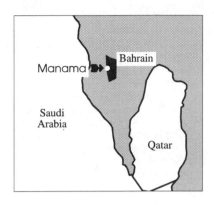

City Significance/History:

Manama the money center, Manama where riches lay hidden. In the land of saltwater and desert sand, fresh water brings life. The city's wealth once richly flowed because of ample fresh water to help date groves flourish and because of pearls lifted out of knee-deep waters.

Now pearl divers have been replaced by urban oil workers; wooden sailing ships stopping to fill their water tanks have become supertankers moving millions of barrels of oil. The wealth continues to grow.

It is expected Bahrain will be the first Gulf state to run out of oil, but they are already planning ahead. Building a supertanker dry dock and an aluminum plant are only a few ways they are preparing for the future.

Riches lay hidden

In Manama, commercial banks were started when the oil revenues flowed. Because of this financial system, it leads the way in banking in the Gulf and is the major banking center between London and Singapore. The economy is strong, and with investments under way, Manama will continue to be a leader in the Gulf.

══ Prayer Points ══

1. Pray that more people will listen to the Christian radio programs beamed into the city, and pray that more Bibles will become available for distribution.

2. Pray that more Christian expatriates will come from Asia to be involved in evangelism and discipleship.

3. Pray that the emir and his advisers will allow evangelism among the Bahrainis.

4. There is one Arabic-speaking evangelical congregation consisting mainly of expatriates. Pray for its witness to the many Muslims.

5. Pray for a spiritual harvest through the distribution of Christian literature and videos.

Kuwait City
(koo-**wayt**)

Day 8

Meaning: "small fort"
Country: Kuwait*
Population: 231,000
Poverty: War has disrupted and reduced the standard of living
Religious Breakdown:
  94.0%   Muslim
  5.3%   Christian (among expatriates)
  0.13%   Evangelical
Status of the church: 25 expatriate congregations, a few national believers
Major Religious Sites:
  Grand Mosque,
  Shabaan Mosque

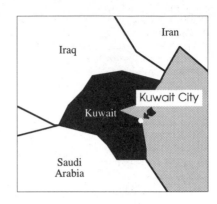

City Significance/History:

From a small desert oasis making money from pearls and other traded goods, Kuwait City exploded as an oil producer. Five gates made entrance into the walled city possible. These walls, once protecting it from invasion, have crumbled. The city has expanded past the old walls, but invaders still attack.

Oil wealth has turned Kuwait into one of the world's richest countries. Schooling, electricity, and water are all free to the Kuwaitis. Iraq's desire for more oil, supposedly to share it with poorer countries, was their justification for military invasion in 1990-91. When the Iraqis were driven out, Kuwait City was free once again. The oil fields were ablaze with 500 wells burning out of control. Black haze blocked the noonday sun. The Persian Gulf was full of oil.

Now the fires have been put out and the city cleaned, but the fear and horror of those days remain in the hearts of the people.

The rebuilding of the city and the return to a normal life has been one of the government's central concerns. Damage to government and historical buildings was extremely high. The physical damage is being repaired, but the people's lives will continue to be affected by the memories of the war.

═══ Prayer Points ═══

1. Since the war physical rebuilding has started; however, emotional rebuilding comes more slowly. Pray for the families torn apart in the violence, as many lost relatives.

2. The war caused many Muslims to question Islam's teaching about life after death. Pray that many would turn to the Resurrection and the Life.

3. Pray for strength and boldness for Kuwaiti believers and for the establishment of an indigenous church.

4. Pray that the emir will grant full freedom of worship and witness to Kuwaiti and indigenous believers.

5. Pray that Kuwaiti money will never again be used to propagate Islam by building mosques, burning Bibles, and paying for Islamic conversions.

Beirut
(bay-**root**)

Meaning: "wells, springs"
Country: Lebanon*
Population: 1,543,000
Poverty: 16 years of civil war have left
    ruin and poverty
Religious Breakdown:
    61.0%   Muslim
    38.0%   Christian (Catholic & Orthodox)
    0.04%   Evangelical
Status of the church: 2000-year-old Orthodox
    and Catholic churches, a few evangelical
    churches
Major Religious Sites:
    Harissa and Mt. Sherbal Maronite Monasteries

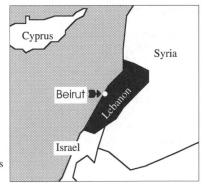

City Significance/History:

A succession of different foreign powers have overrun and controlled Beirut throughout the last 4000 years. The Assyrians, Greeks, Romans, Ottoman Turks, and French all used this city as a regional base. Most of these powers brought their gods with them.

For most of the 20th century Beirut was a beautiful Mediterranean city and recognized as a principle banking and commercial center for the Arab world. Since the 1970s, Beirut has turned into a battle zone, and different sides have taken up arms. The religious lines were set. The Muslims controlled the western side of the city, and the Christians the eastern side. Written cease-fires were nullified when another bomb would explode, renewing violence and fear between both sides.

Peace has returned to Beirut after a decade and a half of war in which Muslims and Christians brutally killed each other. It looked more like the times of the Crusades, rather than the modern age. How long this peace will last is not known. The government is trying to rebuild the infrastructure of the city and country. Investors who helped the city become the Paris of the Near East after World War II have not returned, fearing religious instability and violence.

═══ Prayer Points ═══

1. A greater sense of unity in the body of Christ has developed. Pray that it will continue and increase. Pray also that believers would be strengthened in their faith.

2. Pray that Christians would take advantage of a great openness among non-Christians to hear the gospel.

3. Pray for the youth, that they would not be drawn into immorality and drugs, and that God would open doors for ministry so that youth can be reached.

4. Many families have suffered tremendously, losing members through violence and bloodshed. Ask God for comfort and consolation in the healing process.

5. Pray for the gospel to be preached on radio, TV, videos, and in audio cassettes and literature. Pray also that the church has a greater vision for media ministry.

Tirana
(ti-**rah**-nuh)

Meaning: ancient name of Tuscany
Country: Albania*
Population: 427,000
Poverty: Poorest nation in Europe
Religious Breakdown:
   81.0%   Muslim
   18.0%   Christian
   0.06% Evangelical
Status of the church: A few evangelical
   fellowships have recently started
Major Religious Sites:
   Ethem Bey Mosque,
   Enver Hoxha Memorial

City Significance/History:

Paul, in Romans 15:19, reported that he had "preached the gospel of Christ" in the region of Illyricum, which lays on the Adriatic Sea.

Romans marched through this area on their way to Thessalonica and Constantinople. Other invaders in turn conquered, but were replaced by the Muslim Ottoman Turks. Albania became the only European country to be predominantly Muslim.

Barkinzadeh Suleiman Pasha, an Ottoman Turk, founded Tirana in the 17th century, and it became Albania's capital in 1920. At this time, there were about 12,000 residents living in the city.

During World War II, communism gripped the city and radically changed it. For almost 50 years the strictest communism in the world closed churches and mosques, outlawed all religions, and sealed off the country from the outside world. Party propaganda shaped the lives of the people. The citizens were told that they were the richest people in the world because in other Western countries only a handful of people were rich while the masses were extremely poor.

People's eyes have been opened to the lies. Albanians now realize they are the poorest nation in Europe, with 60% unemployment and rapid inflation.

Prayer Points

1. Pray for the poor as they struggle to live in a post-communist country—that God would use the economic struggles to bring many to himself.

2. Pray that the influence and plans of Islamic nations to "evangelize" Albania would be thwarted.

3. Pray for the improvement of roads so that the gospel can be better transported to villages in the mountain regions.

4. Pray that all the short-term evangelistic work done during the summer will be successfully followed up as planned. Without effective follow-up many young believers will not receive the needed discipleship.

5. Pray for unity among the churches and that the church would find favor with the government.

Cairo
(kI-roh)

Meaning: "the victorious"
Country: Egypt*
Population: 10,361,000
Poverty: Many slums
Religious Breakdown:
   87.0%   Muslim
   12.0%   Coptic Christians
  0.73%   Evangelicals
Status of the church: Home of ancient
   Coptic Church, growing evangelical church
Major Religious Sites: Ibn Tulun Mosque,
   El Ibn el Asn Mosque, Sultan Hassan
   Mosque, Al Azhar Mosque and University,
   El Hussein and Sayida Zeynab Tombs

City Significance/History:

The Bible tells of Jesus being taken to Egypt by his family because Herod was seeking to kill him. Tradition says he went to Cairo. After Jesus' resurrection, the old Roman fortress in Cairo became a Christian colony, church, and eventually, convent. The ancient Coptic church also became centered in Cairo.

In the shadows of the ancient pyramids, Cairo rises from the desert floor as the largest city in Africa. Spreading out along the Nile River over the centuries, the river provides life to a desert land. In the spring the desert heat increases. Sand blows and covers the streets of Cairo.

Islam entered the area early after Muhammad's death, and has been a strong force ever since. Al Azhar founded the oldest university in the world—it developed into the foremost Islamic theological center in 970. The crusaders tried to take Cairo by force, returning Christianity to the area, but were successfully turned away by the Muslim defenders.

For the poor, life is hard. Living in overcrowded, run-down slums, millions are all in the same situation—there is no hope and seemingly no way out. They feel stuck and humiliated—yet their religious pride is still not broken.

Prayer Points

1. Pray for the gospel to be presented to Muslims (most of whom are poor) in an understandable way and for culturally sensitive churches to be planted.

2. Pray that false worship involving homage to dead Muslim saints would be broken and that people would worship the risen Jesus.

3. El Azhar is the largest Islamic university in the world and sends out hundreds of Islamic missionaries annually. Pray that the students would be disillusioned with Islam and turn to Christ.

4. Pray for strong biblical faith in the Coptic and Evangelical churches.

5. Pray for zealous Christian young people to be raised up to evangelize Cairo and Egypt. Pray for the few missionaries already being sent out from Egypt.

Amman
(ah-mahn)

Day 9

Meaning: "protected by Ammon"
Country: Jordan*
Population: 1,273,000
Poverty: Alignment with Iraqis during the Gulf
War hurt the economy
Religious Breakdown:
95.0%   Muslim
4.69%   Christian
0.2%   Evangelical
Status of the church: 11 evangelical churches,
most converts come from the nominal
Christian population
Major Religious Sites: King Hussein Mosque,
Abu Darwish Mosque, King Abdullah Mosque

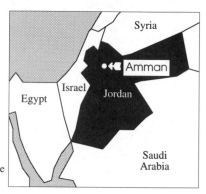

City Significance/History:

This ancient city dates back to the 4th millennium BC. In the Old Testament it is known as the Ammonite city of Rabbah. King David sent Uriah to this city to die in battle to cover David's sin with Bathsheba. At the city's capture David completely destroyed the inhabitants by having them walk through an extremely hot furnace. David was, in some way, following a local custom. For Molech, a deity to whom parents sacrificed their children by having them walk into or pass through a fiery kiln, was the god of the Ammonites.

As a fortified city in almost desert conditions, water is extremely important to life. Caravans of traders would pass through the city, exchanging goods and replenishing water. The city grew slowly over the seven hills of the area. The population exploded when it became the capital of Jordan in this century. Once a major hub of ancient travelers, it continues to be a crossroad in Jordan.

Jordan maintains the sacred Muslim shrines in Jerusalem and paid millions to regild the Dome of the Rock in 1994. Peace talks with Israel have reopened borders between the two nations. King Hussein's American-born wife helps him maintain close ties with the West.

Prayer Points

1. Pray for the important work of Bible and literature distribution. Christian literature is sent from here throughout the Middle East.

2. Pray that the youth of the city (50% of the population is under the age of 15) will have the chance to hear and respond to the gospel. Pray that the camp ministries for these youth will bring many into the kingdom.

3. Pray for continued peace with Israel, which will allow more opportunities for fellowship and ministry with churches in the West Bank.

4. Pray that godly and willing leaders will be raised up to serve growing churches and that finances to support them will be released.

5. Because of the war, 400,000 Palestinians fled to Amman from the Gulf. Pray for ministry to this group which is experiencing poverty and unemployment.

Damascus

Day 9

(duh-**mas**-kus)

Meaning: named after Damshak, the city's founder
Country: Syria*
Population: 2,511,000
Poverty: Increasing hard times
Religious Breakdown:
90.0%   Muslim
8.8%   Christian
0.1%   Evangelical
Status of the church: Christians have the freedom to worship, a number of churches
Major Religious Sites: Omayyed Mosque, Chapel of St. Paul, Takieh es Sulaymanieh Mosque, Tomb of Sayyidah Zaynab

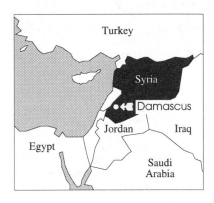

City Significance/History:

On the road to Damascus Paul the apostle's life was forever changed by the power of Jesus. But people lived in the city many years before Paul's visit. Records unearthed in the city indicate that from the 3rd millennium BC to the present, the city has been inhabited.

Because of its location, the city has been conquered, destroyed, and rebuilt many times. Most of the ancient empires controlled the city during their apex. The religion of the city changed with almost every foreign power. The Arameans built a temple to their god, Hadad, the god of storms and rain. In the 3rd century, this same temple site was used to construct an enormous temple for the Roman god Jupiter, the god of war, lighting, and thunderbolts. With the rise of Christianity in the Roman Empire, the temple was converted into the Church of St. John the Baptist. It is believed his head is still at the site.

With Islam's arrival, the church was converted to a mosque, only later to be taken down and rebuilt into the largest mosque of its time (7th century). Two of the Omayyed Mosque's minarets are named the Minaret of the Bride and the Minaret of Jesus. Muslim tradition says that Jesus will appear at this location on the Judgment Day.

Prayer Points

1. Pray that the Orthodox and Catholic Christians would be born-again, active believers and witnesses.

2. Pray for laborers interested in serving among the new slums and unreached poor areas of the city.

3. Pray that the Muslim majority would receive godly wisdom from their Christian contacts and that the conversions out of Islam would increase. Pray for Christians to have boldness when given the opportunity to witness.

4. Pray for effective evangelism through Christian TV and radio—that Bibles and Christian literature would have a greater impact.

5. Pray for more full-time workers to serve the churches and to train new leaders in the congregations.

Gaza
(gozz-uh)

Meaning: "strong, fortified"
Country: Gaza Strip
Population: 1,073,000
Poverty: 73% are refugees
Religious Breakdown:
  98.0%   Muslim
  1.5%   Jewish
  0.39% Christian
  0.03% Evangelical
Status of the church: 1500 believers,
  Greek Orthodox, Baptist, and
  Roman Catholic churches
Major Religious Sites: Said Hashim Mosque,
  Umar Mosque, ibn Uthman Mosque, Church
  of St. Porphyrius

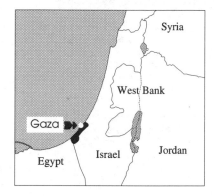

City Significance/History

From ancient times, Gaza has been ruled by the Egyptians, Philistines, Jews, Arabs, and Turks. Biblically it is known as the city of Samson. The British oversaw it until the Arab-Israeli war of 1948 after which Egypt took control of the area.

In 1967 Israel occupied the Gaza Strip. They desired a buffer zone between themselves and Egypt.

Many Palestinian Arabs live in Gaza but work in Israel. Years of violence have led to talks focused on allowing the Palestinians to control the area. Many Palestinians were killed in the Intifada, which protested the Israeli soldiers occupying the territory.

After 27 years of Israeli military occupation, a settlement was reached that set up a Palestinian homeland.

The land is not completely Palestinian because sixteen Israeli settlements with 5000 people yet remain. The settlement is still being worked out, and violence sponsored by the radical group Hamas has not stopped.

In May of 1994, Palestinian limited rule began, but within two days Israeli soldiers were shot at the new border. The political situation remains tense, as Palestinian and Israeli extremist groups work to destabilize the fragile peace.

Prayer Points

1. Pray for Arab pastors who are willing to live and labor in Gaza. With newfound nationalism and the ongoing violence it is an extremely hard place to minister.

2. Pray for increased outreach from the "House of Light" bookstore. If people read God's Word, God will draw them to himself.

3. Pray for peace among the residents, and reconciliation between Arabs and Jews.

4. Pray for a better standard of living to alleviate the poverty.

5. Pray for protection of believers who are caught in the political crossfire—that they would remain strong for the Lord during the hard times.

6. Pray that the Christian social work done in Gaza would effectively demonstrate the love of Christ to the Muslim population.

Jerusalem

(jeh-**roo**-suh-lem)

Meaning: "city of peace"
Country: Israel*
Population: 518,000
Poverty: New immigration has
  stressed the economy
Religious Breakdown:
  72.0%   Jewish
  25.0%   Muslim
  2.34%   Christian
  0.16%   Evangelical
Status of the church: Ancient church, 1,000
  Messianic Jews
Major Religious Sites: Western (Wailing) Wall,
  Temple Mount, Dome of the Rock, Al Aksa
  Mosque, Church of the Holy Sepulchre

City Significance/History:

This holy city is the focal point of the three monotheistic religions—Judaism, Christianity, and Islam. It dates to Abraham's meeting with Melchizedek, the king of Salem, in Genesis 14. Mount Moriah, outside the city, was where Abraham offered his son Isaac on the altar, before God provided the lamb. (Muslims say that it was Ishmael, not Isaac.) Years later, Jesus was crucified outside Jerusalem.

King David built the city as the capital. His son Solomon built the first Jewish temple, later destroyed by the Babylonians in 586 BC. A second temple was built by Zerubbabel and enlarged by Herod the Great. Jesus prophesied its destruction, and in AD 70 the Romans took it apart stone by stone.

Muslims dominated the city for nearly 1300 years. It is their third holiest city and the Dome of the Rock was built on the site of the temple mount. The Crusaders briefly ruled during the 12th century. Mamelukes and Ottomans controlled it until the British occupation during World War I. Jerusalem was reunified again under Israeli rule in 1967.

Christian prophetic expectations are focused on this city of peace. Jesus' second coming to the Mount of Olives is yet to be realized in Jerusalem.

Prayer Points

1. Pray that the veil of blindness would be lifted from the Jewish people and that they would believe their own scriptures in the Old Testament.

2. Pray that God would bond the believing Jews and Arabs together in such love that this would point their peoples to the Messiah.

3. Pray that the spirit of rabbinic Judaism would be bound as the city is perhaps the greatest stronghold of religious spirits in the world.

4. On October 4, the Day of Atonement will be celebrated. Pray for conviction of sin, repentance, and the spirit of grace and supplication to come upon the Jewish people.

5. On October 9-17, the Feast of Tabernacles will be celebrated. Pray that God's faithfulness will be remembered as well as his ability to keep Israel through trials.

Tel Aviv
(tel aveev)

Day 10

Meaning: "hill of springs"
Country: Israel
Population: 2,092,000
Poverty: New immigration has
stressed the economy
Religious Breakdown:
  81.4%   Jewish
  10.0%   Muslim
  2.34%   Christian
  0.16%   Evangelical
Status of the church: Several congregations of
  Messianic Jews and Arab believers
Major Religious Sites: Tel Aviv—Great
  Synagogue; Jaffa—Al Mahmudia Mosque,
  Hassan Bek Mosque, Siksik Mosque

City Significance/History:

The 70 kilometers between Jerusalem and Tel Aviv are as different as night and day. The mountains surrounding ancient Jerusalem give way to the Mediterranean coastal plains upon which the modern city of Tel Aviv was built.

In 1909 some 60 Jewish families sought to create a Hebrew city of their own. Just north of Jaffa (Joppa) they bought land and created Tel Aviv. This new city attracted Jewish immigrants from Europe.

Jaffa is where Jonah caught a ship to Tarshish, and Peter had his vision regarding the spiritual "cleanness" of the Gentiles. Through this ancient port, now engulfed in the rapid expansion of metropolitan Tel Aviv, passed the timbers used for building the temple.

For a brief time, the city was the capital of the new Israeli state and the lifeline for the Jews in Jerusalem during the war of Independence in 1948. Tel Aviv has become the main center for commerce and business in Israel, and its international airport is the gateway to the country.

> **Jerusalem,**
> **the ancient religious city;**
> **Tel Aviv,**
> **the modern secular city**

Prayer Points

1. Pray for unity among the local leadership as well as between the Arab and Jewish believers. Pray that judgment and criticism in the body of Messiah would be gone.

2. Pray that believers would have greater boldness to witness publicly to the residents who are spiritually open.

3. Pray for strategic outreach centers to be established in the city's heart and for more Hebrew-speaking teachers and evangelists.

4. Tel Aviv is the "sin capital" and Jaffa the "drug capital" of Israel. Pray against the remaining Canaanite strongholds such as immorality, hedonism, and drugs.

5. The youth are searching for spiritual reality, often through New Age and occult activity. Pray for an effective strategy to reach the city's young people.

Istanbul

Day 11

(is-tan-bool)

Meaning: "in the city"
Country: Turkey
Population: 10,000,000
Poverty: High inflation and swelling population have stressed infrastructure
Religious Breakdown:
99.8%   Muslim
0.20%   Christian
0.01%   Evangelical
Status of the church:
20 Turkish fellowships, patriarchate of Eastern Orthodox Church
Major Religious Sites: Hagia Sophia, Sultan Ahmed (Blue) Mosque, Suleyman Mosque, Eyup Mosque, Topkapi Palace

City Significance/History

Istanbul's strategic location has been important since its beginning. Dorian Greeks led by Byzas started a fishing village here in 657 BC named Byzantium. The city was razed and rebuilt by the Romans in the 2nd century AD. Constantine captured the city in 324 and made Constantinople the "New Rome." The Byzantines ruled their empire from here for the next 1000 years until the Muslim Ottoman Turks captured the city in 1453.

Istanbul is the only city to span two continents—Europe and Asia with the Bosphorus Strait separating the two. The strait is the gateway between the Mediterranean Sea and the Black Sea.

In 537, Justinian completed the Hagia Sophia—the largest and most beautiful church ever built, standing as a testimony to the Lord Jesus Christ. Like most of the churches in Turkey it was converted into a mosque. To promote religious harmony in the city, it is now a museum.

Istanbul continues to be a strategic city. Industry, commerce, and a major port enhance its importance. Being the largest city in Turkey it sets the pace for Westernization. Its population—already the largest in Turkey—is exploding through rural migration.

Prayer Points

1. Pray that God would use the city's ancient roots as a religious and political capital to reach many throughout the Muslim world with the gospel.

2. Pray for unity and love among the local Turkish fellowships.

3. Pray that the economic crisis will cause Turks to think deeply about the emptiness of pursuing only material gain.

4. Pray that the rise of the fundamentalist Muslim political party will cause nominal, secular Muslims to reconsider what Islam is and who they are.

5. Pray for the development of Christian radio and TV programming, and for the distribution of Christian videos, especially the *Jesus* film. Pray for more people to use the Bible correspondence course to learn about Jesus.

Ankara
(ahng-kuh-ruh)

Day 11

Meaning: "narrow rocky gorge"
Country: Turkey*
Population: 3,000,000
Poverty: 20% unemployment
Religious Breakdown:
   99.8%   Muslim
   0.02%   Christian
   0.01%   Evangelical
Status of the church: Several small Turkish
   fellowships
Major Religious Sites: Haci Bayram Camii
   (Mosque), Ataturk Mausoleum, Kocatepe
   Camii, Hisar Citadel, Temple of Augustus
   (originally a shrine to Cybele)

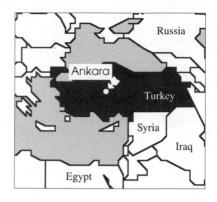

City Significance/History

Throughout its history, Ankara has been a fortified trade center in Asia Minor. Located on the east/west and north/south trade routes, Ankara has shaped political and world history. This crossroads location allowed it to grow and influence many other lands because world news and events traveled with the traders. They would tell stories about what was going on in other parts of the world.

Almost every invading military force conquered and invaded Ankara. The ancient Hittites lived in Central Anatolia. Later, the crusaders fought for the Hisar Citadel, capturing it only long enough to have the Muslim forces drive them out.

Today Ankara has been restored to a city of great importance and world influence. It is now the home of many government offices, embassies, universities, and medical centers. Turkey has an important role in shaping other Central Asian Muslim countries because many of their people share Turkic roots.

> **In 1923 Ataturk declared the city to be Turkey's new capital**

Prayer Points

1. Pray that the Holy Spirit would strengthen the indigenous Turkish fellowships and that as they are strengthened they will witness to the Muslim Turks.

2. Pray that the young elders will mature spiritually and exemplify faithful leadership.

3. Pray that the young, single believers will find Christian spouses so that model Christian homes can be established to draw people to Christ.

4. Pray that the Christians will find good, steady employment to relieve the economic persecution they are suffering.

5. Pray that the large university student population can be reached with the gospel.

6. Pray that the gospel can be seen as the balm to heal the deep divisions in society between religious groups, races, men and women, and rich and poor.

Izmir

(iz-meer)

Meaning: "myrrh"
Country: Turkey
Population: 2,500,000
Poverty: Inflation has stressed the economy
Religious Breakdown:
   99.8%   Muslim
   0.02%   Christian
   0.01%   Evangelical
Status of the church: NATO and expatriate
   congregations, 1 Turkish fellowship
Major Religious Sites: Kadifekale (Mt. Pagus);
   Temple of Artemis (at nearby Ephesus),
   Sadirvanalti Mosque, Hisar Mosque,
   Kestane Pazah Mosque, St. Polycarp's Church

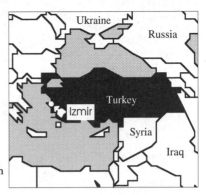

City Significance/History

Birthplace of the poet Homer, Izmir (Smyrna until 1923) is considered one of the most beautiful cities on the Mediterranean Sea. Its strategic location has brought many conquerors— Alexander the Great, the Romans, the Byzantines, and the Ottomans. In 1922 as Ataturk, the founder of the modern Turkish republic, was driving the Greeks out of the city, a disastrous fire broke out that burned most of Smyrna. Until that year there were more Jews and Christians living in the city than Muslims.

A new city arose from the ashes, making Izmir very modern with wide streets and contemporary architecture. It is a busy seaport, connecting Turkey with Europe and Africa. Smyrna is one of the seven churches addressed in Revelation. To the church at Smyrna write:

> I know your afflictions and your poverty…! I know the slander of those who say they are Jews and are not, but are a synagogue of Satan. Do not be afraid of what you are about to suffer. I tell you, the devil will put some of you in prison to test you, and you will suffer persecution for ten days. Be faithful, even to the point of death, and I will give you the crown of life.

St. Polycarp's Church, located in the city, memorializes the martyrdom of the 2nd century bishop, Polycarp.

Prayer Points

1. Pray that the entrenched greed, materialism, and immorality in the city is broken by the power of God.

2. Pray that the new church building can be a protected meeting place for seekers and an open atmosphere where the gospel can be explained clearly.

3. Pray for the students from the 2 universities to come to Christ and to reach out to fellow students.

4. Pray for more Turkish Christian fellowships to develop in the city.

5. Pray for faithful elders, willing to endure persecution, to be raised up to lead the Turkish fellowship.

6. Pray for a peaceful resolution of the Kurdish conflict and for effective outreach to the Kurds.

Baghdad
(**bag**-dad)

Meaning: "God's gift"
Country: Iraq*
Population: 4,511,000
Poverty: Military mobilization has kept the oil wealth from the needs of the people, UN sanctions have crippled the economy
Religious Breakdown:
  95.4% Muslim
   3.3% Christian (mainly Catholic)
  0.03% Evangelical
Status of the church: Orthodox and Catholics have ancient roots, a few evangelicals
Major Religious Sites: Marjan Mosque, Kadhimain Mosque

City Significance/History:

The people after the Flood built an extremely high tower. From the Tower of Babel all the ethnic groups in the world migrated after the confusion of languages. The site later become the city of Babylon, center of the empires of Hammurabi and Nebuchadnezzar. Split in half by the Tigris River, it was world famous for its Hanging Gardens.

Persians, Greeks, and Romans fought for and dominated the area because of the agricultural potential of the fertile Tigris valley. By the 9th century, Baghdad had grown to be almost one million people and part of the predominately Muslim empire of Adu Jafur al-Mansur. His empire stretched from western China to northern Africa. People would travel to Baghdad because it was the educational center of the known world.

Many other powers controlled the area after al-Mansur's empire lost power and wealth. The city went into economic decline and the population dwindled.

In the 1930s, Iraq became an independent country, with Baghdad as the capital. Villagers flocked to the capital to better their life. The Persian Gulf War inflicted heavy damage to the city. Electricity and water systems have slowly been replaced and repaired.

Prayer Points

1. After the Gulf War the government allowed a truckload of Bibles to go into Baghdad. Pray that the Word of God would produce a great harvest.

2. Pray that Saddam Hussein would stop his repression of ethnic minorities and discrimination of Christians.

3. The Muslim majority has recently shown a greater interest in the gospel. Pray for increased evangelistic efforts among the Muslims.

4. The *Jesus* film was shown on national TV in 1991. Pray for its continued showing and distribution, and that a great harvest would result.

5. Pray for revival in the Orthodox and Catholic churches and continued growth in the evangelical house groups.

Tehran
(te-**rahn**)

Meaning: "plain" or "pure, beautiful"
Country: Iran*
Population: 7,509,000
Poverty: Slum communities in and
around the city
Religious Breakdown:
98.0%   Muslim
0.5%   Baha'i
0.4%   Christian
0.03%   Evangelical
Status of the church: Evangelicals are
currently facing great persecution
Major Religious Sites: Aramgah-e Imam
Khomeini (Khomeini's grave), Sepahsalar
Mosque, Armenian Cathedral, King's Mosque

City Significance/History:

Located in the foothills of the Alborz Mountains, Tehran was a little village along the trade routes. With time, a fortified city protected the merchants and travelers. In the late 12th to the 17th centuries, Mongol and Safaid invaders captured and developed the city.

A period of turmoil followed until Agha Muhammad raised an army that conquered the whole of Persia. His capital was Tehran, where he had himself crowned Shah (the monarch of the area). Other shahs took his place as the city continued to develop. Adobe homes were built with little thought to city planning 200 years ago.

As the 20th century arrived, so did modernization. The streets followed a grid system, the population expanded (arriving mostly from rural Iran), and pollution become a rising health concern. The Shah was replaced in 1979 by the Ayatollah, and Iran moved from looking to the West to Islamic fundamentalism.

The Iran-Iraq war forced many people living in western Iran to seek jobs and safety in the capital. Tehran continued to grow, with many slum communities filling the southern suburbs. With the rapid population growth, it is expected that Tehran will soon be one of the ten largest cities in the world.

Prayer Points

1. Several Christian leaders have recently been martyred. Pray that government persecution of the church will end.

2. Pray for the believers to remain bold and full of joy and that constitutional freedoms will be restored as they face increased opposition from the Muslim majority.

3. Pray that this center of Islamic fundamentalism would no longer export its tyranny to other Muslim countries.

4. Pray that missionaries would again be allowed to work in Iran.

5. Pray for the Holy Spirit to renew the traditional Armenian and Assyrian Christian communities.

Mashhad
(mah-shahd)

Day 12

Meaning: "place of martyrdom"
Country: Iran
Population: 2,450,000
Poverty: Migration has increased the number
of poor communities
Religious Breakdown:
99.0%   Muslim
0.2%   Christian
0.02%   Evangelical
Status of the church: A few believers and
churches
Major Religious Sites: Imam Reza Shrine
Complex, Gombade Sabz Mausoleum,
Khwajeh Rabil Mausoleum

City Significance/History:

Mashhad is Iran's holiest city. Back in the 9th century, Imam Reza (the only official imam buried in Iran until Ayatollah Khomeini) was poisoned and martyred in the city. He was the eighth imam (head spiritual leader) of Shiite Islam. His holy position made his tomb a sacred place for pilgrims to worship.

Before he died, the city was known as Sanabad, a small village in the north of Persia. After his death, pilgrims came and ended up staying in Mashhad. The village grew into a small city because of his shrine. Sunni Muslim forces sacked the city, followed by the Mongols in the 13th century. The shrine was badly damaged and, after time, rebuilt.

In the 16th century, three Safavid dynasty rulers established Shi'ite Islam for the whole territory. The shrine was restored, enlarged, and a mosque was built. These rulers made pilgrimages to the site and since then it has become the most holy Shi'ite pilgrimage site in Iran.

A few years ago, a group of religious *mujahidin* started a riot that turned the city into a battle zone. Over 40 people died, and the ones who started the riot were hung by the Revolutionary Guard. A flood, believed to be further punishment, killed even more people seven days later.

════ Prayer Points ════

1. Pray that this Islamic stronghold would be penetrated by the transforming power of the gospel.

2. Pray that Christian radio and videos would be widely received and distributed.

3. Pray that Bibles and Christian literature sent through the mail would reach their destinations.

4. Terrorist acts at religious sites have recently claimed the lives of many pilgrims. Pray that disillusionment would cause seekers to find Jesus.

5. Pray for strength and joy for the believers living in such a hostile environment.

Central Asia

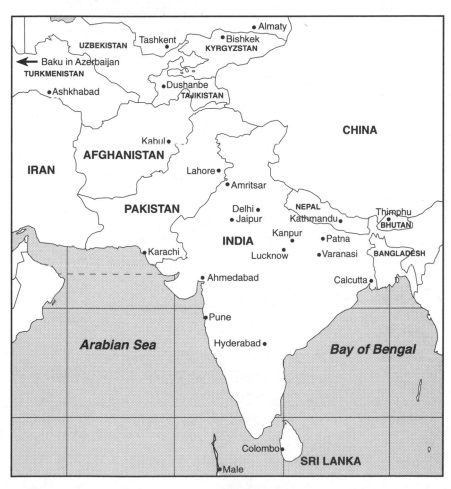

UZBEKISTAN Tashkent ● Almaty
● Bishkek
KYRGYZSTAN

← Baku in Azerbaijan
TURKMENISTAN

●Ashkhabad ●Dushanbe
TAJIKISTAN

CHINA

Kabul●

AFGHANISTAN

IRAN Lahore●

●Amritsar

PAKISTAN Delhi ● NEPAL Thimphu
● Jaipur Kathmandu● ●
BHUTAN
Kanpur
INDIA ●Patna
Lucknow ●Varanasi BANGLADESH
●Karachi

● Ahmedabad Calcutta●

●Pune

Arabian Sea Hyderabad ● Bay of Bengal

Colombo●
SRI LANKA
●Male

24 Cities

CITY	MAJOR UNREACHED PEOPLES
Baku	Azeri, Tatar, Bashkir, Chechen
Ashkhabad	Turkmen, Uzbek, Russian, Kazakh
Tashkent	Uzbek, Tajik, Kazakh, Russian
Dushanbe	Tajik, Uzbek, Korean
Bishkek	Kyrgyz, Uzbek, Russian, Ukrainian
Almaty	Kazakh, Uzbek, Tatar, Russian, Uygur
Kabul	Pushto, Hazara, Tajik, Turkmen *October 15, 1995*
Karachi	Sindhi, Punjabi, Pushtun, Baloch *Oct, 15*
Lahore	Punjabi, Urdu, Hazara, Tajik *Oct, 15*
Male	Maldivian, Sinhalese
Ahmedabad	Central Bhil, Mina, Sindhi, Southern Bhil
Jaipur	Rajasthani, Bangri, Bagri, Wagdi
Amritsar	Sikh, Mina, Urdu, Garhwali
Delhi	Urdu, Kashmiri, Sikh, Mina
Pune	Magadhi Bihari, Berar Marathi, Konkanese
Hyderabad	Deccanni, Bundelkhandi, Gormati, Tulu
Calcutta	Bengali, Hindi, Urdu, Nepali
Kanpur	Awadhi, Bihari, Urdu, Garhwali
Varanasi	Bhojpuri Bihar, Malvi, Maitili
Lucknow	Bhojpuri Bihar, Kanauji, Urdu, Garhwali
Patna	Bhojpuri Bihari, Chattisgarhi, Kortha Bihari, Nagpuri Bihari
Kathmandu	Tibeto-Burma, Nepalese, Maitili, Bhojpuri Bihari
Thimpu	Bhutanese, Drukpa, Nepali
Colombo	Ceylon Moor, Sinhalese, Tamil

86

Baku
(bah-koo)

Day 13

Meaning: "violent winds"
Country: Azerbaijan*
Population: 1,808,000
Poverty: Increased poverty since the
fall of the USSR
Religious Breakdown:

80.0%	Muslim
17.3%	Atheist
2.67%	Christian
0.01%	Evangelical

Status of the church: Russian Orthodox and
Armenian churches, 200 national believers
Major Religious Sites: Lezgi Mosque,
Dzhuma Mosque, Adjarbek Mosque,
Synyk Kala Minaret

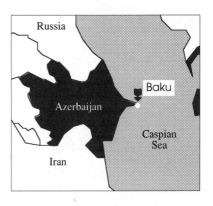

City Significance/History:

Oil pools allowed people to scoop oil out of the ground and worship their god. A perpetual fire was tended by the priests, as Zoroastrians believed in Ahura Mazda, a god who would send his son as a special "expression" of himself to the lower world. It was believed a virgin would bathe in a lake in the east, become pregnant, and give birth to a son.

Baku, a fortified township, rose and fell as different powers marched through the area. The Persians, Muslims, Arabs, Seljuk Turks, Mongols, and Russians all had control over this low-lying city on the Caspian Sea.

Oil, just below the surface, attracted many into the area 100 years ago. By 1901, Baku supplied a little over half of the world's oil. During World Wars I and II, Baku became an object of military importance. Hitler sent troops to conquer the oil fields, but the Russians held them off at Stalingrad.

For seventy years Baku was connected to the USSR, but now they look to their Muslim southern neighbors for trade and economic assistance.

In 1989 an Islamic higher academy, a madrassa, was opened in the city—the first since all were closed in the 1920s.

Prayer Points

1. Nationalistic hopes have fanned an Islamic revival. Pray that freedom of religion will continue and anti-Christian sentiment will diminish.

2. Pray that the youth of the city might hear the gospel and be saved.

3. An Armenian massacre in the city in 1989 has fanned an Armenian independence movement. Pray for the fighting to cease and reconciliation to occur.

4. There are no Azerbaijani congregations. Pray that God will establish an indigenous church and raise up its leaders.

5. Pray that skilled tentmakers will be called to work in the city.

6. The oil fields and wells have caused great pollution. Pray for the people suffering because of polluted water and land.

Ashkhabad
(**ahsh**-kuh-bahd)

Day 13

Meaning: "city-in-love"
Country: Turkmenistan*
Population: 407,000
Poverty: Increased poverty since the
    fall of the USSR
Religious Breakdown:
  76.0%   Muslim
  18.2%   Atheist
   5.7%   Christian
  0.01% Evangelical
Status of the church: Russian Orthodox,
    Baptist, and Charismatic churches, only a few
    Turkmen believers
Major Religious Sites: Behaist's Mosque, Kan
    Abdul Qasim-Babir Mosque (nearby Anau)

City Significance/History:

The name of the city comes from the tale of two lovers who made Allah mad. Allah turned the woman into a river and the man into a city. A desert was placed between them to separate them.

The Kara-Kum Desert, with its scorching heat, made nomadic life difficult. Water could only be found in a few oases towns scattered across the desert. At the Kopet Dag Oasis in the 19th century, the Russians built a stronghold for their trade interests in Persia. They constructed railways across the desert, causing Ashkhabad to become a growing north/south trade center.

In 1948, an earthquake measuring 9 points on the Richter scale shook apart the mud brick homes, leaving only 12 buildings standing and over 100,000 people dead. From the rubble sprang a new and reinforced concrete city.

With construction of the Kara-Kum Canal, which allows water to flow from the Caspian Sea into the desert, Ashkhabad has a large water source that enables large agricultural projects to develop.

This capital city is famous worldwide for its handmade carpets.

> **A family with an old man is a family with a treasure—**
> **Turkmen proverb**

═══ Prayer Points ═══

1. The eldest men in Turkmen society are respected by family and friends. Pray that God will touch these men and that they in turn will spread Christ family to family.

2. Islamic and Turkmen culture had been suppressed by the Soviets—now many are seeking spiritual things. Pray that the search will show them their need for a Savior.

3. Ashkhabad is home to many educated people, who are open to new ideas. Pray for these people to seize opportunities to listen to the gospel.

4. Pray that God will stir an interest in the Russian scriptures available among the Turkmen. Many Turkmen read Russian and can learn about Jesus in the Word. Pray for the translation of the Bible into Turkmen to be completed and effective.

5. Pray for workers to equip the indigenous church.

Tashkent

(tahsh-kent)

Meaning: "city of stone"
Country: Uzbekistan*
Population: 2,037,000
Poverty: Increased poverty since the
fall of the USSR
Religious Breakdown:
  60.0%   Muslim
  35.0%   Atheist
  4.7%   Christian
  0.13% Evangelical
Status of the church: Russian and Korean
  congregations, a few Uzbek believers
Major Religious Sites: Barak Khana Mosque
  and Madrassa, Sheik Zein-ad-Din
  Mausoleum, Rakat (New) Mosque

City Significance/History:

The 4th largest city of the former Soviet Union and the first city of Central Asia, Tashkent sits as a monument to the 20th century in a land of ancient and, in many ways, unchanged peoples.

Almost completely destroyed by an earthquake in 1966, Soviet planners rebuilt Tashkent along a typical Russian city—with tall office buildings, numerous parks, ornate subway system, and tree-lined boulevards. As the capital of Uzbekistan the decisions made in Tashkent influence the entire region.

Before the fall of the Soviet Union in 1991, Uzbeks born and raised in Tashkent often were more comfortable using Russian than the Uzbek of their grandparents. Uzbek, now the official language, has forced many Russian-speaking but otherwise competent professionals to leave the country. With the new currency, the *soom*, and the economy rapidly moved towards hyperinflation, various people started seeking economic salvation in the form of emigration to the West.

In an attempt to hinder the church, local Muslims petitioned the government to force the Protestant churches to stop evangelizing Uzbeks in April 1994. None of the Christian church representatives signed this agreement.

Prayer Points

1. Pray for believers as they face increasing pressure and persecution—for boldness, wisdom, unity, and love.

2. Praise God for what he is doing among the Uzbeks and other nationalities in Tashkent. Ask him to send more laborers into the harvest fields.

3. Pray for the President and his cabinet—for wisdom, and that justice and righteousness might rule and reign in their hearts and in their decrees.

4. As the Islamic capital of Central Asia, all of its Muslim republics look to the *mufti* based in Tashkent. Pray for a dissatisfaction with Islam and an openness to Christianity.

5. Pray for the few Uzbek believers—that a truly indigenous church would develop.

Dushanbe
(dyoo-shahn-be)

Day 14

Meaning: "second night" or "Monday"
Country: Tajikistan*
Population: 620,000
Poverty: Increased poverty since the
fall of the USSR
Religious Breakdown:

82.3%	Muslim
13.2%	Atheist
4.2%	Christian
0.02%	Evangelical

Status of the church: Russian and
Ukrainian churches, a few national believers
Major Religious Sites: Adjnatepe Hill
(Buddhist), Shamaisur Mosque, Khaji Yakub
Mosque, Yakub Charkhi Tomb

City Significance/History:

The Silk Road twisted its way along
the foothills and steppes of the
Pamirs. A mud fortress in the Gissar
Valley rested next to the Dushanbinka
River. Buddhist traders followed the
trade routes from India into Central Asia,
bringing Buddhism with them. The local
people in the 7th century built a 12 meter
high Buddha as a shrine to worship.

Muslim invaders pushed in from the
south to be replaced by others invading
from the north. The small city was of
little interest and remained poor until the
Russians invaded and made the city the
capital of the Tajik Republic. A railway
was built connecting it with the greater
Soviet Union, which brought Russians to
the city to establish it as "Stalinabad."
The name was later changed back to
Dushanbe. The city grew in population as
industries were established. With the
collapse of the USSR came the collapse
of the peace in Dushanbe.

At night, the city turned into a battle
zone controlled by those with the most
weapons. The police remained off the
streets as the civil war for power
continued to grow. Islamic forces,
nationalist, and democratic opponents all
seek to overthrow the Russian supported
(mainly former communist leaders) Tajik
government. The struggle continues.

Prayer Points

1. Pray that the leaders may bring peace to this war-torn city so that the Prince of
   Peace might be proclaimed.

2. The majority of Russian, Ukrainian, and German Christians have emigrated because
   of the strife. Pray for the few who have remained that they will become the core of a
   new multi-ethnic church.

3. Pray that Muslim Tajik will turn to the Lord and workers fluent in the language will
   be raised up.

4. Pray for the dissemination of the newly translated Tajik Bible and the *Jesus* film.

5. Pray that the few Tajik believers would reach out to their fellow Tajiks with love
   and boldness.

Bishkek
(bish-kek)

Day 14

Meaning: "A stick used to whip mare's milk"
Country: Kyrgyztan*
Population: 710,000
Poverty: Increased poverty since the
   fall of the USSR
Religious Breakdown:
  60.0%   Muslim
  27.9%   Atheist
  11.8%   Christian
   0.16%   Evangelical
Status of the church: Russian Orthodox
  comprise the majority, a handful of national
  believers
Major Religious Sites:
  Gogol Street Mosque

City Significance/History:

The massive Tien Shan Mountains separate western China from the steppes of Central Asia. The nomadic Kirghiz living in round *yurts* (tents) would move seasonally with their herds from the mountains to the flatlands. The mountains forced the trade routes to pass along the foothills, and many people desired to control these routes. The Chinese, other Central Asians, Arabs, and Mongols would storm the region seeking control. For most of the past two millennia, others have ruled the land.

Bishkek, also known as Frunze, was only one of many settlements established along the long Silk Road. From these sites, travelers would journey along the trade route and local peoples would buy and sell goods. One khan would gain control, only to be replaced by another in the continual struggle to control this strategic site.

In 1825, a fortress was built along the Chu River valley to protect tax collectors from the Kirghiz Silk Road pirates. The Russians later invaded Central Asia and this small Silk Road fortification was easy prey for them in 1865. Russia established a stronghold and city. While under Soviet control, the area developed as the capital, educational, and economic center for Kyrgyzstan.

Prayer Points

1. Pray that the residual occultism, shamanism, and demonic possession in the culture will be broken.

2. Pray for unity among the immigrant, ethnic Christians. Their divisions have negatively impacted the church's witness.

3. Pray for the developing Kyrgyz church, that it would be truly indigenous and led by godly leaders.

4. Pray that outside workers would use wisdom and discernment in sharing the gospel within a context sensitive to Kyrgyz culture.

5. Pray for the distribution of the Kyrgyz New Testament and other Christian media and literature.

Almaty
(al-**mah**-tee)

Day 14

Meaning: "father of apples"
Country: Kazakhstan*
Population: 1,197,000
Poverty: Increased poverty since the
   fall of the USSR
Religious Breakdown:
   40.0%   Muslim
   32.6%   Atheist
   27.0%   Christian
   0.73%   Evangelical
Status of the church: Russian
   Orthodox, a few new Kazakh fellowships
Major Religious Sites:
   Pushkin Street Mosque

City Significance/History:

Kazakhs take pride in Almaty, the capital city of Kazakhstan, known for its beautiful setting against the Tien Shan mountains. The Silk Road passed through the area, bringing the Mongol hordes from the north, who left their Mongol features and the Muslim religion.

Today Almaty is the governmental, business, and educational center of the country. However, to prevent the disintegration of the country, the Parliament has voted to move the capital from Almaty to the northern city of Akmola by the year 2000. The fall of Communism toppled both religious and political structures, forcing Kazakhs into

an ideological vacuum. Having always been told what to do and believe, Kazakhs now have freedom to choose. Islam attracts some because it provides clear directives on life and supports Kazakh heritage. Other religions and cults are clamoring for allegiance, while secular materialism is successfully winning many hearts. Furthermore, Communism remains a threat—a chameleon which has changed its colors to blend in and survive.

Kazakhs are at an historical watershed. They desire to believe in something after so many years of Communism.

Prayer Points

1. Pray that the communist forces of atheism would be completely eliminated, and pray that this ideological vacuum will not be filled with Islam or some other cult. Pray against the spread of false religions that seek to trap Kazakhs.

2. Many Islamic nations are trying to influence Kazakhstan, and pressure to restrict Christian witness is growing. Pray that the gospel would not be restricted.

3. Pray that Almaty would be a hub where visiting Kazakh leaders, students, and businessmen would find the Lord and then spread his light throughout Kazakhstan.

4. Pray for this nation as it moves its capital—hopefully keeping it from civil war.

5. Pray for the Bible society office that has recently opened and that the entire Bible will be translated into Kazakh.

Kabul
(kah-bool)

Meaning: "straw bridge" or "Cain"
Country: Afghanistan*
Population: 2,051,000
Poverty: Civil war has caused food shortages and increased poverty
Religious Breakdown:
99.0% Muslim
.9% Buddhist
.01% Evangelical
Status of the church: Only a handful of secret believers
Major Religious Sites: Shire of Ali, Khair Khaneh Temple, Asmayi Temple (Hindu), Poli Khisti Mosque, Pious Martyrs Cemetery

City Significance/History:

The memoirs of Babur the Great say Cain built Kabul. Located on a 5000-foot-high basin surrounded by mountains, Kabul developed as a trade center. People would sift the sand of Kabul River seeking gold dust. Surya, a sun god was worshipped with blood sacrifices. The central Asmayi Mountain is named after an eight-armed Hindu goddess of nature (sister of Durga and Kali in India), whose shrine lies at one of the gates of the city.

Kabul has been repeatedly conquered by invading armies such as the Greeks, Mongols, Arabs, English, and Soviets. The Kabul wall was breached by Muslims in the 7th century after being resisted for 100 years.

In 1978 a Communist coup set the stage for the Soviet invasion a year and a half later. The ensuing war left 80 percent of the villages destroyed. During the eight-year Soviet occupation Kabul was protected from destruction. When Najibullah's "puppet" regime fell, the victorious *mujahidin* factions turned on each other and have largely destroyed the city. The vicious fighting between Muslim groups has caused many to question Islam. Different *mujahidin* groups control certain sections of the city. Mortar shells blow out windows and cars are stolen at gun point. Rockets have reduced at least half the city to rubble, and life is cheap.

Prayer Points

1. In 1973 the government destroyed the Christian international church in Kabul, bringing what seems to be a curse over the city and government. Pray that the curse would be turned into the blessing of knowing Jesus.

2. The country is in need of a strong leader. Pray that a godly leader like King Cyrus would be raised up to establish law and order in the city.

3. Pray for disarmament of the many factions and for peace among ethnic groups. Pray for human rights and freedoms to be granted to the people.

4. Pray that God would use this meaningless violence to advance his gospel and for the reconstruction of the city and the return of refugees from around the world.

5. Pray that a viable fellowship of indigenous believers will be raised up in the city.

Karachi
(kuh-**rah**-chee)

Meaning: original name "Kullachi"
Country: Pakistan
Population: 9,506,000
Poverty: Growing because of migration
Religious Breakdown:
  96.0% Muslim
  1.5% Hindu
  2.5% Christian
  1.0% Evangelical
Status of the church: Growing through Christian births
Major Religious Sites: Quaid-i-Azam Mausoleum, Defense Society Mosque, Abdullah Shah Ghazi Shrine (Sufi)

City Significance/History:

Until the mid-19th century, Karachi was only a small fishing village and fort wedged between the Arabian Sea and the expanse of desert to the north. At the time, the British were gaining interest in the area. They built a naval base and moved the territorial capital from Hyderabad to Karachi.

Railways connecting it with the north were built, the port expanded, roads were paved, and Karachi became a place of migration for the first time. The population grew quickly. As the capital and commercial center, many people relocated to the area after massive irrigation projects turned the hot dry desert into farm land.

In 1963, the capital of Pakistan was moved to the planned city of Islamabad. Karachi, the main port city for the country, continued to be the commercial center. Islamabad is conservative, with many women in veils and traditional black garb. Karachi, in contrast, has Western dress and is more liberal.

Water supply in the desert is always a problem. The water system in Karachi has become insufficient for the expanding population.

Karachi's most impressive monument is the tomb of Muhammad Ali Jinnah, the man who led the country to independence and served as the first governor general.

Prayer Points

1. Pray for effective ministry to the 1 million drug addicts in the city.

2. Pray for evangelization of the Mohajirs, Ismaili Muslims, and Afghan refugees.

3. Pray for the salvation of 1 million Balochs in the city; there are only 10 known Baloch believers in the world.

4. Pray that inter-ethnic conflicts, kidnappings, and violent crimes in the city will cause people to look to Jesus for answers.

5. Pray that the few Pushtu-speaking believers can boldly declare the gospel to the 2 million Pukhtun people in the city.

6. Pray that the church would be healed of divisions and delivered of Hindu superstitions and occultic practices, and that pastors would be strengthened.

Lahore
(luh-**hore**)

Meaning: "iron" –suggesting fortification
Country: Pakistan, Punjab Province*
Population: 4,926,000
Poverty: Many are poverty-stricken
Religious Breakdown:
- 95.0%   Muslim
- 0.5%   Hindu
- 3.5%   Christian
- 2.0%   Evangelical

Status of the church: Growing with a few large, visible fellowships
Major Religious Sites: Sunehri Mosque, Badshahi Mosque, Wazir Khan Mosque, Data Ganj Bakhsh Hajveri Mausoleum, Masjid-e-Shuhuda

City Significance/History:

Built on the trade routes between the Indian subcontinent and Central Asia, Lahore has seen many battles. Invading forces have repeatedly fought over the city, which has been the capital of the Punjab for over 1000 years. The Ravi River provides all the water needed for its hot arid environment. A massive canal was built for irrigation, allowing the city to spread out along its banks.

In the 11th century, Islamic forces took control of the city. Muslim factions battled for it over the following centuries. The Moghul rulers in the 16th century made it into a Islamic center for learning and the arts. The walled Lahore Fort, built in 1560, became the city's main defense. Its repeated destruction and rebuilding testifies to the city as a battleground. In 1770 Lahore was sold to a Hindu Sikh ruler and later the British took control. With the independence of Pakistan in 1947, the city returned to Islamic leadership.

Karachi is the commercial center, Islamabad is the political center, and Lahore is the cultural center. As the cultural center, it is the protector of Islamic ways and traditions. The Shalimar Garden, built by Shah Jahan in 1642, is a popular place for escaping the extremely hot summer months.

Prayer Points

1. Pray that those who practice folk Islam, worshiping the city's patron saint, would hear the good news of Jesus Christ.

2. Pray for the protection of new believers who undergo persecution mainly by relatives because of their faith.

3. Pray that backbiting, politics, and corruption would no longer hinder the church's witness and that harmony, purity, and unity would instead characterize the church. Pray for church leaders to lead the way in this.

4. Pray that the provincial assembly in Lahore would have God-fearing representatives making godly decisions for the welfare of the province and country.

5. A number of Christian organizations have their headquarters in the city. Pray for wisdom for their leaders and for effectiveness in their ministry in the city.

Male
(mah-lee)

Meaning: "mountain"
Country: Maldives*
Population: 50,000
Poverty: Most people live at subsistence levels
Religious Breakdown:
99.4% Muslim
0.5% Buddhist
0.1% Christian
Status of the church: No officially recognized Maldivian believers
Major Religious Sites:
Grand Friday Mosque, Hukuru Mosque

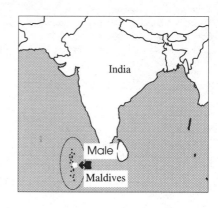

City Significance/History:

Little is known about the ancient history of Male. It is believed that the small island nation of the Maldives was founded by sailors from India, Sri Lanka, and other countries.

It is likely that the people worshiped the sun as their god, with beliefs also in evil spirits. Because most of the 1192 islands are only a meter or two above sea level, ancient temple sites have been converted into mosques. Most mosques in the world are built with their main wall facing Mecca; in the Maldives when the Muslims pray, they face the corner of the mosque because the old foundations face the sun.

Islam entered the country in the 12th century when Arab and North African merchants established control. By the 16th century, the Portuguese desired more influence in the East Indian trade, and built a fort at Male. They replaced the existing Muslim sultan and expanded their dominance. The sultan's followers rebelled and massacred the Portuguese.

The sultan firmly established Islam as the state religion, and Islam has continued to be the only religion of the area. Male has been protected by other rulers, but never completely controlled by outside powers.

Prayer Points

1. Pray that Bibles and Christian literature may be legally imported, and that examination of incoming mail will end.

2. Pray that Bibles in the Dhivehi script will become available and that anti-conversion laws will be changed.

3. Pray that the suspicion of and prejudice against Christianity might be removed.

4. Pray that restrictions against Christian media might be lifted and that the gospel may be heard. Pray that Christian radio programming will be developed.

5. Pray that tentmakers will be able to obtain residency visas to work in the city.

6. Pray that Christian expatriates will have wisdom and discernment when and how they should share the gospel with the city's residents.

Ahmedabad
(ah-**med**-uh-bahd)

Meaning: "Ahmed's town"
Country: India, Gujarat Province*
Population: 4,396,000
Poverty: 41% slum dwellers
Religious Breakdown:

75.0%	Hindu
10.93%	Muslim
5.0%	Sikh
3.58%	Christian
0.52%	Evangelical

Status of the church: 63 churches
Major Religious Sites: Jami Masjid Mosque,
Sidi Saiyad Mosque, Ahmed Shah Mosque,
Hathee Singh Temple, Hathee Singh Temple

City Significance/History:

Ahmad Shah I, sultan of the Gujarat state of western India, founded the city early in the 15th century. The city found life along the Sabarmati River, where he built the city on the site of Karnavati. Karna was a Hindu god—the son of the Sun and Pritha. It was said that Karna was born clothed with arms and armor. He was later killed in a battle, and his religious fame died with him.

With the city's name change also came a strengthening of Islam. Mosques were built and Islam grew stronger. The Jami Masjid Mosque was constructed from the demolished Jain Temple. Tensions between Hindus and Muslims continue. Mahatma Gandhi longed for a peaceful unification of the two religions. From Ahmedabad he walked to the Indian Ocean in protest of the Salt Laws. However, the rise of the BJP, a radical Hindu political party, has threatened to destabilize the country's political life and social balance. The BJP is threatening the freedom of minority religions.

The city is one of India's most important textile centers. Yet it has a huge slum population, which possesses no or inadequate civil amenities. Most people are illiterate and unemployed, and street children are the byproduct of this tragic situation.

Prayer Points

1. The Hindu Navariati festival has also attracted many Christians, adversely affecting their faith. Pray that believers would be renewed by the Holy Spirit.

2. Pray that the united peace march by the churches and the "Love Ahmedabad Project" would demonstrate Christ's love to the Hindus and Muslims who are in conflict.

3. The city is a stronghold of the BJP. Pray that this radical Hindu party would lose its political influence and stop its opposition to Christianity.

4. Pray for outreaches to the vast slum population and to the two universities.

5. Pray that the government will continue to allow religious freedom.

Jaipur
(ji-poor)

Meaning: "city of victory"
Country: India, Rajasthan Province*
Population: 1,969,000
Poverty: 108 slums
Religious Breakdown:
    89.0%   Hindu
    7.5%   Muslim
    0.41% Christian
    0.05% Evangelical
Status of the church: 26 churches, some 8000
    Christians with half of south Indian origin
Major Religious Sites: Iswari Minar
    Swarga Sul, Jantar Mantar Observatory

City Significance/History:

Three ancient forts rest on the hills overlooking most of present-day Jaipur. Well water allowed this desert oasis to grow on a dried lake bed. The Amber Fort was the capital of the Mina tribe, who were the original inhabitants. The Jaigarh Fort, containing India's largest cannon, was so impregnable that no enemy breached its walls.

In 1727, Maharaja Jai Singh II planned the expansion of the forts to one large fortified city. The city expanded and a wall was built around it with seven gates. At night, the city gates were closed for protection. On the outside of the gates, long anti-elephant spikes were mounted to keep enemies from using their elephants to ram the gates.

The color pink was said to be the color of hospitality. When Britain's Prince Albert visited the city in 1883, all the main buildings were painted pink to welcome him. As the provincial capital, Jaipur has continued to keep its traditional pink color.

The wall has been torn down and used to build homes, yet the gates remain. The wall's foundation marks the old city, but Jaipur has expanded outside the old walls. Camels still pull carts down the street as Jaipur keeps its old and new moving together.

Prayer Points

1. Pray that the Muslim Meo people might become responsive to the gospel. Among the Muslim Meo people are no known Christians.

2. The higher caste Hindus—the Rajputs, Jats, and Marwari—have shown little interest in the gospel. Pray that the spiritual powers keeping them in darkness will be broken.

3. Pray for increased conversions through literature distribution, radio evangelism, and Bible correspondence courses, and that the number of churches would multiply.

4. Worship of rats produces conditions that foster pneumonic plague. Pray that the idolatry underlying this health hazard would be bound.

5. Most children in Rajasthan are married at age eight. Pray that laws abolishing child marriages would be obeyed.

Amritsar

(ahm-rit-ser)

Meaning: "pool of immortality"
Country: India, Punjab Province
Population: 837,000
Poverty: A few slums
Religious Breakdown:
   60.7%   Sikh
   36.9%   Hindu
    1.1%   Muslim
    1.1%   Christian
    0.5%   Evangelical
Status of the church: Roman Catholics
   make up the majority, a few evangelicals
Major Religious Sites: The Golden Temple,
   Durgiana Temple (Hindu)

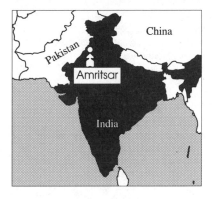

City Significance/History:

Hinduism has been in India for thousands of years. Islam entered in the 12th century, converting many in the north. Violence between the groups has been widespread ever since. In an attempt to unify the two religions, a new religion was started—Sikhism— in the 15th century by the Guru Nanak. One hundred years later, the fourth Sikh guru founded Amritsar as a holy Sikh city. It quickly became the center of the Sikh religion.

A temple built next to the pool of nectar was destroyed by the Mongol invaders and later rebuilt, this time coated with copper. This Golden Temple is the holiest of all Sikh temples.

When Gandhi was seeking the peaceful withdrawal of the British, Amritsar became the site of one of the largest Indian massacres. The British, trying to establish control in the Punjab, opened fire on the Indians. In an attempt to survive the flying bullets, many Indians jumped into the city's main well. The British killed or wounded over 2000 Indians. Even with Indian independence, peace has not come.

In the last decade, the Indian Army has had to fight the Sikh extremists who have taken the Golden Temple as a fortress. The extremists desire an independent Punjab state for Sikhs.

Prayer Points

1. The Christians are underprivileged, generally nominal, and discouraged. Pray that the Holy Spirit would renew and refresh the believers.

2. Violence and killing by Sikh extremists have terrorized the city. Pray that these events would open the hearts of the people to the gospel.

3. Many caste groups as well as tribal groups are unevangelized. Pray for workers to take the good news of Jesus to these people.

4. Pray that pilgrims to the Golden Temple would instead find the Lord Jesus as Savior.

5. The Sikh holy scripture, the Granth Sahib, is located in the Golden Temple. Pray that its influence would be replaced by God's Word, the Bible.

Delhi
(del-ee)

Meaning: "threshold"
Country: India*
Population: 10,857,000
Poverty: 3.5 million people in slums
Religious Breakdown:
 52.0% Hindu
 25.0% Muslim
 20.0% Sikh
 0.9% Christian
 0.01% Evangelical
Status of the church: 220 congregations
Major Religious Sites: Jama Masjid Mosque,
 Lakshmi Narayan Temple, Might of Islam
 Mosque, Nizam-ud-din Shrine

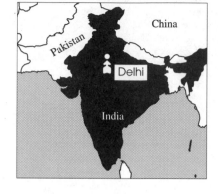

City Significance/History:

Delhi has been a hub of activity since the 4th century B.C. Traders would come and go to the old city. In the 12th century, Delhi became the capital of Muslim India. The Moghul invaders brought bloodshed and Islam with great force. At this time, most of northern India was under Moghul power. The Red Fort was built to protect the city and to display the glory of the Moghul Empire.

The capital has moved to a number of other cities until the British built New Delhi. Old and New Delhi are a mixture of culture, style, and history.

Delhi, the capital of India, displays the diversity and contrasts of a third-world urban center in the process of modernization. Imported cars and colorful city buses share the streets with horse-drawn carts and wandering cows. People of varying languages, educational levels, and cultures migrate here from all over India. They are drawn by the economic and educational opportunities. Temples of all shapes and sizes, scattered steeples of ancient churches, and myriads of mosque minarets reflect the religious diversity.

The capital has mushroomed in size since the British left. Air pollution, high electricity usage, and water shortages have become growing problems.

Prayer Points

1. Pray that peace and love would replace the spirit of violence and anger in the city.

2. Pray that God would use the government in Delhi to allow more freedom for Christian witness throughout all of India.

3. Little outreach is focused on the Hindus, Muslims, and Sikhs. Each group needs its own church. Pray for workers to be raised up to plant churches.

4. Modernization has strained the city to the limit, with vehicle pollution choking everyone. Pray that the growing disillusionment will turn people to Jesus.

5. Pray for aid and outreach to the 3.5 million people who live in the growing slums.

6. The headquarters of many Christian organizations are here. Pray for wisdom for the leaders so that spiritual blessings might flow throughout the country.

Pune
(poo-nuh)

Meaning: "city of merit"
Country: India, Maharashtra Province
Population: 2,971,000
Poverty: 6 slums
Religious Breakdown:
  80.4% Hindu
  10.0% Muslim
   2.5% Christian
   1.0% Evangelical
Status of the church: 59 churches
Major Religious Sites: Mahadji Mausoleum,
  Qamarali Darvesh Mosque, Pateleshwar
  Temple, Parvati Temple, Shinde Chhatri
  Temple, Saras Buag Ganesh Temple

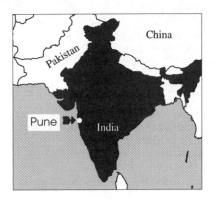

City Significance/History:

The Creator and Destroyer Shiva is one of the main gods of Hinduism. For those who worship him, he is the supreme god; there is no other. He is the power of opposites, creator—destroyer, controls good—evil, and gives rest—ceaseless activity.

Shivaji, a great Hindu political leader in the 17th century, derived his name from Shiva. Shivaji was born in Pune and led battles of unrest against the Muslim Mongols. From Pune, once the capital of the Hindu Maratha Empire, many Hindu social reform movements were launched against the Muslim powers. In the 18th century, a temple to Shiva was built as a stronghold of Hinduism.

The British captured the city in the early 19th century, and turned it into a place to retreat during the monsoons and heat of Bombay. They developed the city into a major educational and cultural center—"the Oxford of India."

In 1985 Bhgwan Rajnnesh was found guilty of immigration fraud charges. Forced to leave the USA, he finally ended up in Pune. Teaching a progressive Hinduism, he was not greatly accepted by Indian Hindus. He died a few years later. Many of his followers from other countries still flock to Pune to pay homage to their dead spiritual master.

Prayer Points

1. Pray for unity among the small Protestant community, particularly that all would have a personal experience of salvation.

2. Pray for spiritual renewal among the large minority of Catholics, and pray for growth and outreach in the few evangelical churches.

3. Pray for ministry among the high population of Jains who are largely unevangelized.

4. Shiva grips the hearts of the Hindus living in the area. Pray that Hindus would turn to the loving Father.

5. Pray that Western pilgrims visiting Rajnnesh's grave would find the living Lord.

6. This educational center attracts many foreign students, mainly African. Pray for workers and outreaches to the universities.

Hyderabad
(hI-der-uh-bahd)

Meaning: "lion town"
Country: India, Andhra Pradesh Province*
Population: 4,208,000
Poverty: Many slums
Religious Breakdown:
- 85.5%   Hindu
- 8.47%   Muslim
- 2.9%   Christian
- 1.0%   Evangelical

Status of the church: 134 churches from different denominations
Major Religious Sites: Birla Mandir Hindu Temple, Mecca Masjid Mosque, Charminar Mosque, Mahan Kali Temple

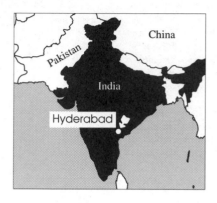

City Significance/History:

Hinduism was replaced by Islam, only for Hinduism to regain control again—one spiritual power rising against another. As Islamic Moghuls gained power in the north, they sought to control India's south. Islamic raiding parties went to Golkonda to capture it. The solid stone walls of its citadel held off the warriors for 8 months, but finally fell to the Moghul forces.

The citadel increased and expanded in the 16th century to create a new city, Hyderabad. Hyderabad became a regional center for Islam and seat of the wealthy Nizam (ruler) of Hyderabad. The Nizam ruled the area from the 18th century until the British displaced their rule.

In 1947 independence was granted to India by the British. The Nizam tried to gain control again by calling for an independent Islamic territory. But 85% of the city's population was Hindu at the time, and the Indian government in Delhi did not want a separate Islamic state within India.

Today Hyderabad has grown, connecting itself with the neighboring city of Secunderabad. Together, this metro area comprises India's sixth largest city.

As the provincial capital, it is also home for one of the largest Christian populations in India.

Prayer Points

1. Pray that the minds of believers would be renewed, so that unbiblical thinking that has persisted in the traditional Christian community would cease.

2. Pray that the believers would become involved in cross-cultural evangelism and for a harvest among the largely unreached Muslims.

3. Pray that the Christian agencies, institutions, and teachers here would have a great spiritual impact on the city.

4. Vacation Bible Schools are being used to reach children. Pray for many children and parents to come to Christ.

5. Many beggars are in the city. Pray for them to come to Christ and to find work.

6. Pray for the vibrant pastors' and leaders' fellowship to grow and affect the city.

Calcutta

(kal-**cut**-uh)

Meaning: after the goddess Kali
Country: India, West Bengal Province*
Population: 13,604,000
Poverty: World's lowest urban living standard,
  400,000 homeless
Religious Breakdown:
  75.5%   Hindu
  22.9%   Muslim
  (1.5%   Christian
  0.03%   Evangelical
Status of the church: 163 congregations,
  only 45 Bengali-speaking
Major Religious Sites: Kali Temple,
  Sitambara Jain Temple, Tara Keshwar Temple
  Nakhoda Mosque, St. Paul's Cathedral

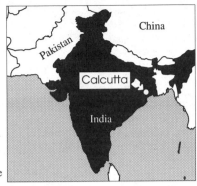

City Significance/History

A little over 300 years ago, Calcutta was just one of thousands of small villages in India. The British in the late 17th century settled here, and the village quickly grew into a city. Invasions by Indians made it necessary for the British to build a fort for protection. Calcutta became the capital and export center. William Carey pioneered a missionary movement here in 1793. The fall of the British caused great hardship in the city. Just to the east, East Pakistan (now Bangladesh) was established. Hindus moved west and Muslims moved east.

The slums of Calcutta have been made famous by the humble Mother Teresa. She and others, like the Buntains, have brought hope and life to the slums, but increased migration to the city keeps the slums growing.

The local Bengali people worship Kali. Seen as the Earth Mother-Creator, she also has an evil side. Kali, translated "black," is the goddess of warfare, pestilence, blood sacrifice, and death. Calcutta, the city of Kali, lives up to its name. Many people come here to find a better life; most end up never finding it. Kali with her necklace of human heads claims another victim to death. Yet the masses of people still come. Calcutta is India's largest city—a city deep in bondage to its goddess.

Prayer Points

1. The slums are some of the worst in the world. Pray that the poor can live in dignity and find the food they need. For most the struggle for daily survival allows them no time for spiritual things.

2. The destructive god Kali is worshiped and appeased. Pray that God's power would be evident to the people living in bondage to Kali.

3. Pray that the value of human life, especially of females, will be recognized.

4. Pray for the Christian relief agencies, especially the hospitals and orphanages, that are ministering to the needy. Pray for strength and resources for the staff.

5. Pray for a Christian witness in the city's slums and among the unreached Muslims.

6. Pray for the students studying in the Bible colleges.

Kanpur
(kahn-poor)

Meaning: "ear city"
Country: India, Uttar Pradesh Province
Population: 2,378,000
Poverty: Many slums
Religious Breakdown:
   77.8%   Hindu
   18.6%   Muslim
   3.53.% Christian
   0.34% Evangelical
Status of the church: 37 fellowships
Major Religious Sites:
   JK Glass Temple, Memorial Church

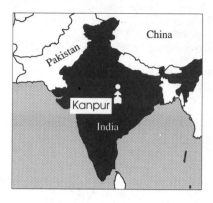

City Significance/History:

From early on, northern India has been a Hindu territory. Millions of different gods and goddesses are worshiped and feared. The Mongol invaders brought Islam with them and some of the people started to follow Islam. Kanpur was a city where a larger number of Indians turned to worship Allah.

Located on the holy Ganges River, Kanpur was a stronghold for the Indian mutiny in 1857 against the British. One uprising against the British saw the Indians massacre and dismember the

The cow is one of the most sacred gods

British. As British forces recaptured control of the city, they inflicted much of the same treatment back on the Indians. They made them drink blood and eat beef—the cow is one of the most sacred gods for Hindus. They fed pork to the Muslims, which is considered extremely unclean by them. All this was done in retaliation for the uprising against the British rule.

Today the city has grown in size and has become one of the largest industrial cities in India.

Prayer Points

1. The few Christian workers here are laboring under very difficult circumstances. Pray for more evangelists and church planters to work in the harvest.

2. Pray that the Muslims, who are a large minority, may be reached with the gospel.

3. Most Christians are nominal and some are reverting to Hinduism. Pray that the knowledge of Jesus as Savior and Lord would grip their hearts.

4. Pray that the students in the city may hear the gospel and respond.

5. Pray that the residents of this spiritually dark province who migrate to Kanpur for work would encounter the gospel and come to faith in Jesus Christ.

Varanasi

(var-uh-**nah**-see)

Meaning: "the city between two rivers"
Country: India, Uttar Pradesh Province
Population: 1,193,000
Poverty: Many slums
Religious Breakdown:
   79.8%   Hindu
   19.6%   Muslim
   0.12%   Christian
   0.08%   Evangelical
Status of the church: 11 churches
Major Religious Sites: Durga Temple,
   Golden Temple, Great Mosque of
   Aurangzeb, Sankatmochang Temple,
   Visvanatha Temple

City Significance/History:

Varanasi (also known as Banaras or Benares) has been a holy pilgrimage site for over 2000 years. Ten kilometers away at Saranath is where Buddha first preached on enlightenment. Hindus flock the ghats (the wide stairways) which provide access to wash, bathe, and even die in the Ganges River.

Relatives carry their dying loved ones to the river. Laying the frail bodies on one of the lower ghats, they place the feet of the dying into the water. When the person dies, it is believed that they will go straight to heaven. This is important to many Hindus, who believe their dead relatives can come back as evil spirits to haunt them. Along one section of the ghats are the cremation pits. After the body has been cremated, the ashes are sprinkled on the holy Ganges River. Pilgrims will bathe in the holy and polluted Ganges, seeking to be healed.

Many Hindu priests live in Varanasi. As they walk around in deep trances, people seek them for blessings. Gurus have students coming from all over India to sit under their teaching, to meditate, and to learn Sanskrit.

Here the main Hindu god is Shiva, the god of life and death, who has power to kill or to heal.

Prayer Points

1. Pray that this holy city of Hinduism would become filled with the presence and power of the Holy Spirit.

2. Pray that the tiny minority of Christians, most of whom are nominal, would experience spiritual strengthening and renewal.

3. Pray that the millions of pilgrims visiting the Ganges River would find the living water given by Jesus.

4. Hindus here are among the world's most unreached mega-peoples. Pray for workers to labor in this vast harvest field. Pray that the leaflets and Gospels that have been distributed would produce spiritual fruit.

5. Pray for a work to be established at the large Hindu university. Little ministry is being done among the students there.

Lucknow
(luck-now)

Meaning: "sign" or "mark"
Country: India, Uttar Pradesh Province*
Population: 1,391,000
Poverty: Many slums
Religious Breakdown:
   76.8%   Hindu
   19.6%   Muslim
   2.7%   Christian
   0.4%   Evangelical
Status of the church: A few mission agencies, 26 churches
Major Religious Sites: Bara Imambara (Shi'ite grave site), Aurangzeb Mosque, Jami Masjid Mosque

City Significance/History:

The Muslim Moghuls established a growing power center in the area. They were replaced by still another Muslim group, the Oudh.

Along the Gomti River arose a small capital city for the Oudh Nawab rulers. These rulers came from a Persian background, not Mongol. From here, the Nawabs controlled north-central India for 100 years. They developed the arts, fine culture, and traditional craftsmanship.

The British annexed the area in the mid-19th century. The backlash from this annexation was an Indian uprising against the 3000-strong British diplomatic presence, including women and children. The Indians far outnumbered the British, who held out for three months in their compound, the Residency of the Nawab rulers. (The Residency was built for the glory of the Nawab rulers.) The Indian onslaught ended when more British troops broke through the Indian lines; however, 2000 of the British were dead.

Today the city still has a devoted Islamic population. Shi'ite holy men of the past are believed to have special power, even in their graves. Many Muslim people pray for strength and blessings at the tombs of these holy men.

Prayer Points

1. Pray for growth in the small churches and that new believers can be taught and discipled.

2. There is an open door for evangelism at several strategic locations. Pray for a harvest to come from the bold witness at these sites.

3. Many East Asian Muslims come here to study. Pray for the establishment of a ministry to them.

4. Pray for reconciliation between the Muslims and Hindus and that the religious tensions would dissipate.

5. Pray for the workers seeking to reach the various people groups in the city.

Patna
(pat-nuh)

Meaning: "pale red son"
Country: India, Bihar Province*
Population: 2,209,000
Poverty: A few slum communities
Religious Breakdown:
- 70.0%   Hindu
- 20.0%   Muslim
- 3.0%   Sikhs
- 4.0%   Catholics and Anglicans
- .01%   Evangelical

Status of the church: 100 believers in a few churches
Major Religious Sites: Har Mandir (Sikh), Sher Shahi, Mahavir Mandir (Hindu),

Husayt Shah Mosque

City Significance/History:

Founded in the 6th century B.C., Patna is the third oldest city in India and a provincial capital. Over the centuries it has seen the rise and fall of major Indian empires, as well as a flow of various world religions.

Geographically it occupies a strategic site, south of where the Ganges River meets two other rivers. This location provided a natural protection. The city was originally founded as a fort, from which it could ward off attacks and raid enemy territories.

Patna has been the seedbed for religions. Besides fostering Hinduism, it berthed an offshoot—Jainism. The city has played a key role in the development of Buddhism, as it is only 100 kilometers from the place where Buddha reportedly reached "enlightenment." Under the reign of Ashoka (3rd century B.C.), Patna became the center for the spread of Buddhism throughout Asia. Over 1000 years later, Muslims used it as a base to propagate Islam.

Today Hinduism is the predominant religion. Muslims make up about one-fifth of the population and the rest are Sikhs, Jains, and Buddhists. There are a few Roman Catholics and Protestants but among these few know Jesus personally.

Prayer Points

1. In light of the city's religious history, pray that God would birth such a mighty movement of his Holy Spirit that Patna would again influence the entire subcontinent—this time for Jesus' glory.

2. "In India, nine out of ten Muslims who convert to Christianity revert back to Islam," declared a Christian leader in Patna. "The family and community pressure is too strong." Pray that the church would provide strong support and fellowship when Muslims turn to Christ.

3. Pray that the strife between Muslims and Hindus would cause disillusionment, leading them to the true Prince of Peace.

4. Pray that the hold of unemployment, poverty, and illiteracy would be broken and that people would be more responsive to the gospel.

Kathmandu
(kat-man-doo)

Meaning: "one temple by a tree"
Country: Nepal*
Population: 372,000
Poverty: Many living below poverty line
Religious Breakdown:
    89.0% Hindu
    7.0% Buddhist
    0.58% Christian
    0.56% Evangelical
Status of the church: 56 churches,
    some growing fellowships
Major Religious Sites: Pashupatinath Temple,
    Talejo Temple, Bodhanath Stupa,
    Swayambhunath Stupa, Kaba Aye Pagoda

City Significance/History:

Trade routes from Tibet and northern India passed through the high Himalayas and flowed past the foothills, where the fertile Kathmandu valley became an important trade center.

By the 17th century, the local Newari people refined much of the Hindu temple and worship art. The valley consisted of small city-states competing to outdo each other in art techniques and creativity. Many of the carved gods and temples took shape during this period.

100 years later, Nepal was unified by the first Gorka king. From this time, the metro area of Kathmandu grew as more and more villagers came from all over Nepal, the vast majority being Hindu.

The Bagmati River cuts through the valley on its way through the foothills of Nepal and meets the Ganges River many kilometers later. Along the river is Pashupatinath, the most holy Hindu temple in Nepal. Pilgrims from India will come here because it is the holiest Shiva temple in the world. Shiva, the creator, the shepherd—Shiva, the destroyer, the bloodthirsty, is who the pilgrims seek. Protecting the entrance to Shiva's temple is Nandi, Shiva's golden bull.

Not many kilometers to the west, the Great Stupa of Bodhanath is the largest Buddhist temple in Nepal.

Prayer Points

1. Pray for the removal of the barriers to Christianity in the minds of Hindu Nepalis.

2. Pray that the government would continue to guarantee freedom of religion and that the church could evangelize without persecution.

3. The churches in the Kathmandu valley are clannish and divided. Pray that they would become unified in Christ.

4. Pray that the believers would be delivered from superstitions and old ways of living and that they would learn to walk in the Spirit.

5. Pray that the caste system, which separates people, would be brought down.

6. Pray that the spiritual fire begun by the A.D. 2000 Congress on Evangelism in Kathmandu would continue to burn throughout the country.

Thimphu
(tim-poo)

Meaning: unknown
Country: Bhutan*
Population: 121,400
Poverty: Undeveloped subsistence
   economy, development potential
Religious Breakdown:
  70.1%   Buddhism
  24.0%   Hindu
  5.0%   Muslim
  0.33%   Christian
  0.21%   Evangelical
Status of the church: A few small fellowships
Major Religious Sites: Tashichho Dzong,
   Chang Ganka Monastery, Cheri Monastery

City Significance/History:

All throughout the Himalayas flags and other pieces of cloth wave in the wind as Buddhist prayers continue to be offered by the moving cloths. This small Buddhist country with its largest city and capital, Thimphu, has been left alone throughout history.

During the British occupation of India, British diplomats came through Thimphu seeking permission to move goods from Tibet through Bhutan into India. For periods of time there was no problem being part of this trade route. After the English left and China entered Tibet, Bhutan became a hidden country with Buddhist temples and monasteries dotting the mountains.

In Thimphu is the largest Buddhist center in the country, Tashichho Dzong. The name translates something close to "the fort of the glorious religion." (Similar dzongs are found throughout the country.) One half of the building is dedicated to Buddhism; the other half is used as a government center. From Tashichho, all the civil and religious administration is carried out for the whole country. From here the government is run out of the king's ornate throne room. A Buddhist monastery is also found at this dzong.

Prayer Points

1. Tashichho Dzong is the power center of the country, administrating both religion and government. Pray that God would be known by the monks and political leaders.

2. Pray that the king would be favorable to Christianity and grant freedom to witness and worship. Pray that tentmakers could work without restrictions.

3. Pray for the protection of Bible translators and that translations into Dzongkha, Kebumtamp, and Sharchagpakha would be completed.

4. The Drukpa majority is strongly Buddhist with less than 200 known believers. Pray for a dynamic indigenous church to be raised up.

5. Little Christian literature and no radio programming is available in the official Dzongkha language. Pray for the development of these essential tools.

Colombo

(koh-**lum**-boh)

Meaning: "harbor"
Country: Sri Lanka*
Population: 2,345,000
Poverty: 65% slums
Religious Breakdown:
　70.3%　Buddhist
　14.3%　Hindu
　　7.8%　Muslim
　　7.6%　Christian (mainly Catholic)
　0.44%　Evangelical
Status of the church: Stagnant growth
Major Religious Sites: Kelaniya Raja Maha
　Vihara Temple, Vajiraramaya Temple,
　Grand Mosque

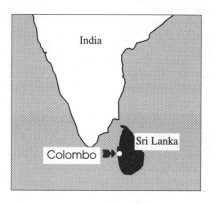

City Significance/History:

Christian tradition holds that the Apostle Thomas visited the area. Maritime Arabs in the 8th century established a port in Colombo for the export of cinnamon. Eight centuries later, the Portuguese replaced the Arabs and traded everything from cinnamon to elephants. The wide variety of spices attracted most traders.

The Portuguese, who brought Roman Catholicism, carved their seal of arms on a rock above the sea and built a fortress. The Dutch and British controlled the area until the British granted Sri Lanka independence in 1948. The growth of the city occurred during the British occupation, as the city continued to develop as a hub for Indian Ocean trade.

The city has become a refuge for the poor of Sri Lanka. Twenty years ago, Colombo's population was only 500,000. Now over 65% of the metro population live in shanties where living conditions are extremely poor. As the city grows, the poor are forced to live next to the canals and roadways. They are moved into the marshes and lowlands, where health conditions are poor. One of the problems facing the government is child labor. Many poor families sell their children to the rich. These children work as domestic help, with the hope that they will receive food and clothing.

Prayer Points

1. Pray for an increase in the standard of living so parents can support their children. Pray that the children who must work for the rich will not be exploited.

2. Pray for protection and strength for the believers who are caught in the political crossfire between the Buddhist Sinhala and Hindu Tamil.

3. Pray for a renewed sense of calling in the national church and that evangelism and discipleship would replace compromise and nominalism.

4. Conversions among the Buddhists and Hindus have produced a backlash. Pray that opposition and persecution would not hinder the ongoing witness to them.

5. Pray for unity and cooperation among evangelicals so the spiritual thrust begun in the 1992 Navodays Conference would truly be the "Dawning of a New Era."

Eastern Asia

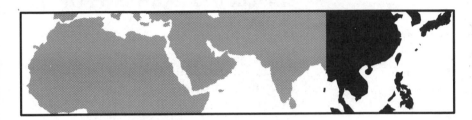

33 Cities

CITY	MAJOR UNREACHED PEOPLES
Taipei	Taiwanese, Hakka, Ami, Paiwan
Shenyang	Manchu, Korean, Mongolian, Hui
Changchun	Manchu, Korean, Hui, Mongolian
Urumqi	Uygur, Kazakh, Hui, Kirghiz
Lhasa	Tibetan, Blang, Bui,
Lanzhou	Hui, Tibetan, Dongxaing
Beijing	Han Chinese, Hui, Manchu
Hohhot	Mongolian, Hui, Manchu
Tianjin	Han Chinese, Hui, Manchu, Bai
Taiyuan	Han Chinese, Hui, Manchu
Jinan	Han Chinese, Korean, Manchu, Mongolian
Nanjing	Zhaung, Yao, Dong, Miao
Xian	Han Chinese, Hui, Manchu
Chengdu	Han Chinese, Yi, Tibetan, Miao
Chongqing	Han Chinese, Yi, Tibetan, Tujia
Shanghai	Han Chinese, Hui, Bai
Wuhan	Han Chinese, Tujia, Buyi, Hui
Guangzhou	Han Chinese, Li, Zhaung, Yao
Hanoi	Vietnamese, Central Khmer, Muong, Hmong
Vientiane	Laotian, Tai, Khmer, Hmong
Phnom Penh	Khmer, Vietnamese, Cham, Mnong
Bangkok	Northern Thai, Southern Thai, Northern Khmer, Pattani Malay
Yangon	Burmese, Burmese Shan, Mon, Yangbye
Dhaka	Bengali, Sylhetti Bengali, Bihari
Kuala Lumpur	Malay, Chinese, Sarawak, Tamil
Jakarta	Buginese, Sasak, Achehnese, Rejang
Bandar Seri Begawan	Malay, Han Chinese, Iban
Ulaanbaatar	Mongolian, Kazakh, Uighur
Pyongyang	Korean, Chinese
Sapporo	Japanese, Eta, Ryukyuan, Ainu
Tokyo/Yokohama	Japanese, Eta, Ryukyuan, Okinawan
Osaka/Kobe/Kyoto	Japanese, Eta, Ryukyuan, Ainu
Fukuoko/Kita/Kyushu	Japanese, Eta, Ryukyuan, Ainu

Taipei
(tI-pay)

Meaning: "north Taiwan"
Country: Taiwan*
Population: 3,561,000
Poverty: Economic stability
Religious Breakdown:
   70.4%   Chinese Folk Religions
   24.2%   Nonreligious/Atheist
   5.0%   Christian
   2.13%   Evangelical
Status of the church: Stagnation in
   church growth
Major Religious Sites: Lungshan Temple,
   Hsing Tien Temple, Temple of Confucius

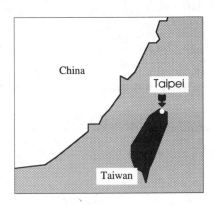

City Significance/History:

The Chinese, as early as the 17ᵗʰ century, sailed to Taiwan and relocated in Taipei. As the Japanese expanded their influence southward, they made Taipei one of their administrative and economic centers. By World War II, it had grown but remained mainly an agricultural hub where three rivers join.

After Japan was forced to surrender, the Chinese Communist movement continued to grow on mainland China. So the Nationalist Chinese, led by Chiang Kai-shek, were forced to retreat from the mainland to Taiwan. Taipei was chosen as the capital and the city expanded. Universities and industries grew quickly as post-war peace gave rise to new hopes and dreams. Many wealthy Chinese fled in fear of the Communists taking all their wealth. These people invested in the development of the new city and nation.

Wise investments and development of industry and educational centers increased the wealth still farther. These advances attracted the rural population. In response, the government started building educational and industrial centers in other cities. This has helped to discourage villagers from relocating. But most still view Taipei as the city of gold, where riches can be found.

Prayer Points

1. Pray that a spirit of sophistication that rejects Christianity can be broken among the young people, so that witness among students will be fruitful.

2. Pray for the political transition occurring in the midst of serious social problems, especially drug abuse.

3. Pray for unity in the church and that national pastors and leaders will be raised up.

4. Pray that the goals of the Year 2000 Gospel Movement will be realized, with the church experiencing much growth and renewal.

5. There is a resurgence of Buddhism and animism. Pray that those who are seeking spiritual reality will find Jesus.

Shenyang
(shen-yahng)

Meaning: "north bank of Shen River"
Country: China, Liaoning Province *
Population: 5,493,000
Poverty: Communism has provided basic needs
Religious Breakdown:
   59.1%   Nonreligious/Atheist
   30.1%   Chinese Religions
   6.1%   Christian
   2.0%   Evangelical
Status of the church: TSPM 82,000 members
   (see Jinan for TSPM explanation)
Major Religious Sites: North Tomb (Beiling),
   East Tomb (Dongling), Gugong
   Imperial Palace

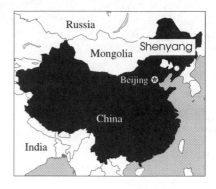

City Significance/History:

Shenyang is the historic cradle of the Manchu people. It was an important city for trade back in the 11th century.

One reason the Great Wall of China was constructed was to protect the Ming Dynasty from foreign invasion. During the 17th century, the Manchus became a formidable and well-organized force, coming from China's northeast. The Ming reign was weakening, and the Manchus were able to conquer the whole country with very little opposition. Many of the leaders that were part of the Ming leadership were killed or submitted to the Manchus. The city became the Manchu capital in 1625.

The Manchus were different—the men shaved their foreheads and a long pigtail flowed down their backs. The Manchu Dynasty (also called the Qing Dynasty) lasted almost two centuries, expanding China's borders to greater lengths than before.

In the 20th century, the Russian and Japanese both occupied the area and started to develop the city as an industrial giant. The city's population exploded because of the converging of six railroads and the industrial expansion.

Prayer Points

1. Qigong, a combination of Chinese martial arts and occultic practices, is making a comeback. Pray that students attracted to the supernatural power which Qigong promises will instead find the power of the Holy Spirit.

2. Pray for unity among the city's believers and that God will expose the false believers within the church.

3. Political motives and connections motivate the older leaders in the Three Self Patriotic Movement. Pray that the younger leaders who seek to preach the gospel will prevail in the current power struggle.

4. Pray that the police will no longer harass and detain these young Christian leaders.

5. Pray that those migrating to the city for work will encounter the gospel.

Changchun
(chahn-chun)

Meaning: "eternal spring"
Country: China, Jilin Province *
Population: 2,620,000
Poverty: Communism has provided basic needs
Religious Breakdown:
59.1%	Nonreligious/Atheist
30.1%	Chinese Religions
1.4%	Muslim
6.1%	Christian
5.0%	Evangelical

Status of the church: TSPM 36,000 members
Major Religious Sites:
Weihuaninggong Imperial Residence

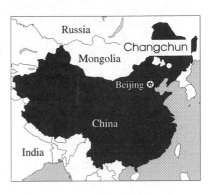

City Significance/History:

Watchtowers top the many buildings of the tree-lined avenues of Changchun. Most of these buildings were built by the Japanese during their military occupation of this region from 1933–45. The city was used for administrative headquarters and the capital of the Manchukou, a "puppet" government set up by Japan. Most of the electric lines were run underground to better protect them during this extremely traumatic time. The Japanese slaughtered many Chinese during their occupation.

The arrival of the Cultural Revolution brought persecution of Christians, and churches were closed. Recently restrictions for churches to minister have been somewhat lifted. Few believers want to identify with the "official" church because of fear of persecution. House churches continue to meet.

Today Changchun is known for its university and automobile industry. It is the site of one of China's most famous film studios.

Because of its proximity to North Korea, the population of Koreans living in the city is significant. When militant communism started to grip Korea, many Koreans fled across the border into the Jilin Province.

Prayer Points

1. Pray for the growing church among the ethnic Koreans in and around the city and that they would zealously share their faith with unreached Koreans in the area.

2. Pray for the ethnic Korean Christians as they seek to contact family and friends back in North Korea. May they bring a bold witness to them.

3. Pray that the film industry would produce pro-Christian films.

4. Pray that Christian radio programming that is broadcast into the city would bring in a great harvest.

5. Pray that Bible study and teaching materials would become available to explain the gospel to students and professors at the university.

Urumqi
(oo-**rum**-chee)

Meaning: "pleasant meadows"
Country: China, Xinjiang Province *
Population: 1,724,000
Poverty: Communism has provided basic needs
Religious Breakdown:

59.1%	Nonreligious/Atheist
30.1%	Chinese Religions
1.4%	Muslim
6.1%	Christian
5.0%	Evangelical

Status of the church: TSPM 4,000 members, 25 known Uygur believers
Major Religious Sites: Hongshan Pagoda, Tianchi (nearby sacred lake), Bogda Feng (nearby sacred mountain), Mingde Church

City Significance/History:

In the far northwestern region of China, the people still have Mongol features, but Islam has traditionally been their religion. The Uygurs, one of the area's ethnic peoples, have a mixture of Chinese and Turkish features.

Throughout most of history, Urumqi was a small dusty Uygur village with little significance, part of the Silk Road.

At the end of World War II, the Communists started to change the look of the village. Concrete-block apartment buildings were built to provide housing, and smokestacks marked another factory on the wastelands at the edge of the

> **Outsiders are controlling a foreign land.**

desert. The Communists sent more than 5 million Han Chinese into Xinjiang Province, China's largest political unit, to dilute the Uygur's nationalistic feelings. During the Cultural Revolution of the late 60s they destroyed thousands of mosques. These are being rebuilt today, but few Uygur young people attend the mosque.

The region has become a nuclear test site, so the presence of the military has increased. Because of this, more Han have relocated here, and they now dominate government, industry, and business, a fact resented by the Uygurs.

Prayer Points

1. Pray for openness to the gospel among the 13 ethnic minorities, particularly the Muslim Uygurs, Kirgiz, and Kazaks. Pray for reconciliation between these minorities and the Han Chinese who comprise 75 percent of the population.

2. Pray that the Han believers evangelize their Muslim neighbors and accept them, despite government pressure.

3. Muslim converts are subjected to great persecution and rejection. Pray that Uygur fellowships would be established for strength and support.

4. Pray for spiritual strength, encouragement, and open doors to witness for foreign believers who have made their home in this remote city.

5. Pray for the completion and distribution of the New Testament and the distribution of the *Jesus* film in Uygur.

Lhasa

(lah-suh)

Meaning: "city of god"
Country: China, Xizang Province (Tibet)*
Population: 120,000
Poverty: Communism has provided basic needs
Religious Breakdown:

   90.0%   Buddhist
   6.1%   Traditional Religions
   2.0%   Muslim
   0.9%   Christian
   0.05% Evangelical

Status of the church: A few small fellowships
Major Religious Sites: Potala Palace;
   Jokhang Temple; Sera, Drepung,
   and Nechung Monasteries

City Significance/History:

The ancient religion of Tibet was Bon, a form of Shamanism. A shaman became a medium between the visible and invisible world. According to Bon, the world had three spheres: heaven, occupied by the Lha (gods), earth, mastered by Nagas (humans), and the underworld, inhabited by Tsen (demons).

The Potala Palace, built in the 17th century, remains one of the earth's most amazing structures. It embodies the heart of Tibetan Buddhism, both as a religion and a political force. Thousands of rooms house shrines, statues, and tombs of former Dalai Lamas. (The Dalai Lama is the traditional government ruler and the highest priest or god. However, after the Communist takeover in 1950, the Dalai Lama moved to India in 1956.) The palace is full of different idols having spiritual significance. Maitrya is an enlightened Buddha yet to come, the wrath of Tara can be sought, or Amitayus will bring infinite life. These are only a few of the idols that find refuge, worship, and honor in this palace.

Rising early in the morning, monks and pilgrims climb the many stairs of the palace chanting, kneeling, rising, walking a step–kneeling, rising, walking a step… chanting the same prayer over and over.

Prayer Points

1. Pray for the salvation of the Karmapa, considered to be the reincarnation of the Great Living Buddha and part of a demonic sect in Buddhism.

2. Pray that Christians in exile will return and preach the gospel and encourage the believers—that the Dalai Lama exiled in India would come to know Jesus.

3. Pray for open doors and wise distribution of the Tibetan scriptures.

4. Pray that Yama, the king of hell who is the demonic protector of Tibet, would be exposed so that many would turn to Jesus, the conqueror of death.

5. Pray that monks initiated into the Tantra of Yamantaka at the Jokhang Temple would come into contact with the Living Word and receive salvation.

6. Pray that the small house fellowships in the city would be strengthened and multiply throughout the Lhasa valley.

Lanzhou
(lan-jow)

Meaning: "the fragrant city"
Country: China, Gansu Province *
Population: 1,803,000
Poverty: One of the poorest areas in China
Religious Breakdown:
   59.1% Nonreligious/Atheist
   30.1% Chinese Religions
   1.4% Muslim
   6.1% Christian
   5.0% Evangelical
Status of the church: TSPM church at
  Zhangye Road
Major Religious Sites: White Pagoda,
  Temple of the Town Gods,
  Blingisi Buddhist Caves

City Significance/History:

Dust rises and blows over the city from the arid desert that runs from Lanzhou into Inner Mongolia. This haze, mixed with industrial pollution, covers the city—the capital of one of China's poorest provinces.

For historic traders crossing the desert, oasis villages provided stepping stones on their way from places as far away as Rome to find the valuable silk of the East. Lanzhou has been a crossroads city from the beginning. The trade routes went in all directions, bringing unusual travelers through the city. Silk went west with travelers; Buddhism was brought up from the south.

Lining the Yellow River, Lanzhou developed as a railroad link for goods going to other places, but it has now been transformed into an industrial center for northwest China.

The Yellow River provides water to desert-like, but extremely fertile land. Crops of melons and fruits keep most of the population working, but in recent years China's atomic energy industry has been based in Lanzhou.

China's atomic energy industry headquarters

Prayer Points

1. Pray for the gospel to come in power to this desolate desert region of China which is spiritually barren as well.

2. Pray for Christian teachers and workers to come to this city, which has low literacy levels and a high poverty rate.

3. Pray for a witness to the Hui people, who are ethnically Chinese but culturally Muslim, and that their traditional resistance to the gospel will be broken down.

4. Pray for the Holy Spirit to move among the Chinese soldiers who make up a large percentage of the population.

5. Pray that the leaders in this provincial capital would not persecute believers and hinder the growth of the church.

Beijing
(bay-**jeeng**)

Meaning: "northern capital"
Country: China*
Population: 12,332,000
Poverty: Communism had provided basic needs
Religious Breakdown:
    59.1%   Nonreligious/Atheist
    30.1%   Chinese Religions
    1.4%   Muslim
    6.1%   Christian
    0.1%   Evangelical
Status of the church: Growing TSPM and
    underground churches
Major Religious Sites: Fayuan Si Temple, Niu
    Jie Muslim Temple, Guangii Temple,
    Mao Zedong Memorial Hall, Temple of Heaven

City Significance/History:

Beijing's location on the edge of China's Northern Plain made it a strategic military location for the control of China's north. Brutal invasions have struck Beijing throughout history.

Genghis Khan, coming down from Mongolia, slaughtered and destroyed the the city in the 13ᵗʰ century. From the rubble arose Khanbaliq, "Khan's Town." His grandson, Kublai Khan, ruled all of China, his capital being Khanbaliq. Corruption and fraud destroyed the Khan's reign, and the Ming Dynasty grew in its place.

The Forbidden City, the Temple of Heaven, and the Ming Tombs are lasting examples of the grandeur and exclusionist attitude of the Ming power base. Reigning from the 14ᵗʰ – 17ᵗʰ century, the Ming Dynasty fell apart, allowing the Qing Dynasty to take over China and set up their capital in Beijing, only later to become a victim of the Cultural Revolution in 1911.

After the Japanese were defeated in World War II, Mao Zedong took power and started the People's Republic of China, turning all of China over to communism. Beijing grew, the old imperialism gave way to communism; with communism came roads, railways, one language, and universal education.

Prayer Points

1. From Beijing 1.2 billion people are governed. Pray for God's purposes to be worked through the government, especially when the communist "old guard" dies. Pray that officials favorable to Christianity will be raised up.

2. Pray for the safety of persecuted house church leaders who seek to minister for Christ in this tightly controlled environment. Pray that believers will have discernment about how and to whom they should share the gospel.

3. Pray that disillusioned university intellectuals in their search for truth would discover Christ. Also, pray for the effective follow-up and nurture of returned intellectuals who have become Christians while studying abroad.

4. Many foreign business concerns are streaming into Beijing. Pray that Christians will wisely take advantage of these opportunities in a way that advances the kingdom.

Hohhot
(hoh-hott)

Meaning: "green city"
Country: China, Inner Mongolia *
Population: 1,312,000
Poverty: Communism has provided basic needs
Religious Breakdown:

59.1%	Nonreligious/Atheist
30.1%	Chinese Religions
1.4%	Muslim
6.1%	Christian
5.0%	Evangelical

Status of the church: 2,000 Mongolian Christians in China
Major Religious Sites: Wuta Zhao (Five Pagoda Temple), Da Zhao Temple, Xilitu Zhao Temple, Great Mosque

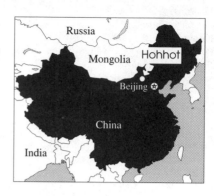

City Significance/History:

The winter was cold as wind blew a fresh layer of snow against the north side of the *yurt* (a nomadic tent home). To avoid the cold, horses were tied on the south side of the small circular home. Inside the goats' milk was still warm. Ogadai remembered the summer when the grasslands provided plenty of food. Now the northern wind blows and almost everything is iced up. Tomorrow he will leave his family and trek the day's journey to Hohhot. He heard a Tibetan Buddhist monk was in town, and he wants to offer a goat to the sun god.

Gods are everywhere—in the rivers, stars, sun, and moon. Nature offered infinite gods to worship and revere. But in Hohhot, Mongol priests know how to make an offering acceptable to the different gods. The Buddhist monk also might be able to offer spiritual insight. In Hohhot, Ogadai can also trade skins for salt and other goods.

Such was the life of a nomadic Mongol herdsman a thousand years ago. Hohhot started as a trading post and a place of temples. As China and the former USSR fought over Mongolia, Inner Mongolia became part of China, with Hohhot being the administrative and educational center. Mongols are a minority people in their own homeland.

Prayer Points

1. Pray for the gospel to be planted and bear fruit among the historically resistant Mongols. Pray for the production of a Mongolian-script New Testament.

2. Pray that radio ministry directed to the Mongols might have an increased harvest.

3. Pray that the nationalistic aspirations of the Mongols might be realized in the coming of the kingdom of God to their people.

4. Illiteracy has been an obstacle to the Han Chinese Christians growing in their faith. Pray for increased understanding of God's Word among these believers.

5. Pray for teachers to help raise the literacy level of the residents.

Tianjin
(tiyen-jeen)

Meaning: "ford of heaven"
Country: China
Population: 10,995,000
Poverty: Communism has provided basic needs
Religious Breakdown:

    59.1%   Nonreligious/Atheist
    30.1%   Chinese Religions
    1.4%   Muslim
    6.1%   Christian
    5.0%   Evangelical

Status of the church: TSPM 78,000 members
Major Religious Sites: Grand Mosque, Dabeiyuan Monastery, Confucius Temple, Tianhou Temple

City Significance/History:

Dating back to the 3rd century B.C., when China's history was known as the Warring States period, Tianjin has had a militant reputation. Many saw this fortified city as strategic because it was ideal as a trade port and the main link with Beijing. France, Britain, Belgium, Germany, Russia, Japan, Italy, and the USA ruled Tianjin because of their interest in Far East trade. For periods, some of these countries had a significant military and diplomatic presence in the city at the same time.

Missionaries, who arrived with the business community, saw the city as an open place to minister.

The foreign invaders all left their mark on the city. Different buildings have French, German, or Italian features. Japan, during World War II, helped the city move forward as an industrial giant.

The Hai River allowed for ships to travel to the city, but heavy silting moved the main port downstream. The Japanese started dredging and expanding the port with the work finally being finished by the Communists. Now Tianjin handles a great number of goods, making it one of the busiest areas in China. It is the country's third largest city and busiest shopping center, with Commercial Street servicing almost 700,000 shoppers daily.

Prayer Points

1. Pray that the Christians will grow in boldness and faith, and that believers holding political positions would have wisdom and an effective witness.

2. Pray that evangelization resources and workers from within and without the country will be called to Tianjin, and that the city might truly become a gateway to the kingdom of heaven in that region of China.

3. Pray that the response to Christian radio broadcasts and the *Jesus* film would greatly increase and that Christian literature would become more accessible.

4. Pray that disillusionment with communism and ancient practices would be replaced with hope in Jesus Christ.

5. Pray that the Christians working among the oil rig workers in the Bohai Sea would have an opportunity to evangelize their coworkers.

Taiyuan
(tI-oo-wahn)

Meaning: "great plain"
Country: China, Shanxi Province *
Population: 2,596,000
Poverty: One of China's poorest provinces
Religious Breakdown:
  59.1% Nonreligious/Atheist
  30.1% Chinese Religions
  1.4% Muslim
  6.1% Christian
  5.0% Evangelical
Status of the church: TSPM 108,000 members
Major Religious Sites: Chongshan
  Monastery, Yongzhou Monastery, Jinci
  Temple Complex, Twin Pagoda Temple

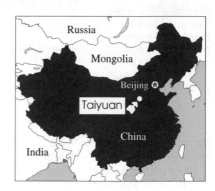

City Significance/History:

From its earliest foundations the city has been a place of conflict. Twenty-seven of the temples at one time were dedicated to the god of war—violence was prevalent. As one military campaign after another swept through China, Taiyuan was always in the way. Almost every invading force conquered the city.

In the early 1900s, the emperor of China gave an edict that all foreigners should be killed, and the Boxer Rebellion was under way. To carry out the edict, soldiers from the Chinese secret society traveled from city to city killing foreigners, especially the "evil ones"—missionaries.

When the troops arrived at Taiyuan, they found a walled city. The gates were closed—trapping everyone inside. The troops hunted down and beheaded the evil ones; 130 foreign missionaries were martyred. But the 3,000 member Chinese local church lost even more, as many of them tried to protect the missionaries or wanted to identify with Christ and not the Rebellion.

Taiyuan is the industrial center of the region, and home to 9 institutes of higher learning.

Prayer Points

1. Pray that from the blood of the martyrs a strong and faithful witness will grow and produce fruit of righteousness greater than the evil of the past.

2. Shanxi Province is one of the least evangelized provinces in China, possibly less than one percent Christian. Pray for evangelists to be raised up and that Taiyuan would become a center for the dissemination of the gospel.

3. Pray for the safe delivery of Bibles and Christian books which come through Taiyuan on their way to believers in the surrounding countryside.

4. Pray for believers enduring extremely harsh conditions in the coal mines around the city, that their joyful witness would draw others to Christ.

5. Pray that worship of Guanyin, the goddess of mercy, at the Chongshan Monastery would be replaced by worship of the true God of mercy.

Jinan
(jee-nahn)

Meaning: "south of the River Ji"
Country: China, Shandong Province*
Population: 3,208,000
Poverty: Communism has provided basic needs
Religious Breakdown:

59.1%	Nonreligious/Atheist
30.1%	Chinese Religions
1.4%	Muslim
6.1%	Christian
5.0%	Evangelical

Status of the church: TSPM 20,000 members
Major Religious Sites: Thousand Buddha
Mountain, Shentong Monastery,
Divine Rock Temple

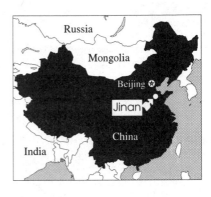

City Significance/History:

Jinan is often referred to as the city of springs, a reference to its 102 natural springs. Their source is the Lake of Great Purity outside the city. Huge dikes protect the city from the Yellow River's periodic flooding. The Shanghai to Beijing railway runs through Jinan, providing income and trade.

In China there are two main distinctions in the church: the Three Self Patriotic Movement (TSPM) and the house church movement. The TSPM is government-controlled and makes worshipers officially register. Because of the government affiliation

In China there are two main churches

with this church, many feel they have sold their souls to the enemy. There is no doubt the government places pastors in the TSPM churches, but true believers do exist in it.

In the last few years, a TSPM seminary has opened in Jinan. Chinese Christians do desire to be trained in leading the church. Over 200 people applied for the 54 openings at the seminary. Around 60% of the curriculum is considered biblical, 40% nonbiblical. Where the Word of God is restricted, prayers need to flow that the 60% would be a sharp two-edged sword.

Prayer Points

1. The government has begun to allow Bibles to be printed in China, most of which go to the spiritually hungry believers in the TSPM churches. Pray that these Bibles will produce a great harvest and true worshipers.

2. Pray for the TSPM seminary. May God use this building and these students to increase his name and glory in all of China. Pray for biblical teaching and training.

3. Pray that residents of this city of springs may come to know the source of the real Living Water, who brings true righteousness and purity.

4. Pray for spiritual revival in this educational and industrial center.

5. Tai Shan, one of China's five sacred mountains, rises 100 kilometers south of the city. Pray that the spiritual power behind this stronghold would be broken.

Nanjing
(nahn-jeeng)

Meaning: "southern capital"
Country: China, Jiangsu Province*
Population: 3,073,000
Poverty: Province called "rice bowl of China"
Religious Breakdown:
    59.1%   Nonreligious/Atheist
    30.1%   Chinese Religions
    1.4%   Muslim
    6.1%   Christian
    5.0%   Evangelical
Status of the church: TSPM 106,000 members
Major Religious Sites: Linggu Temple, Qinhuai
    Confucian Temple, Ming Tomb and Sun
    Yat Sen Mausoleum, Fuzimiao Confucian
    Center, Revolutionary Martyrs Monument

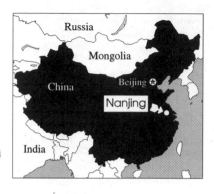

City Significance/History:

As its name suggests, Nanjing has been the capital of China in the past. For economic and military reasons, the city has been selected and rejected as the capital. In the 19th century the Taiping Revolution, a Chinese Christian army, succeeded in controlling most of southern China—only to have the Qing Dynasty, with the help of foreign powers, halt the revolution.

The church continued to grow, but with the Cultural Revolution the church went largely underground. Fear of death or imprisonment, and suspicion of the TSPM's connection to the government, sent many believers into hiding. Small house churches met in many different locations, worshiping quietly and in fear. For almost 50 years, the house church movement has continued to grow. The "official" number of believers is mainly a count of the members in the TSPM. The number of house church believers is not known. Hunger for the Word of God is strong. In and around Nanjing, Bibles will be torn apart, one believer taking the book of John, another Ruth or Hebrews. These extremely poor believers will raise money so that Bibles can be brought in from Hong Kong and other locations.

══ Prayer Points ══

1. Pray for the students and faculty at Jingling Union Theological Seminary, that they would desire to serve God and would be open to his leading.
2. Ask God to bless the correspondence and extension courses offered by the seminary for believers in towns and villages around China.
3. Pray for increased production of Bibles by the TSPM-affiliated Amity Foundation, and that these would get into the hands of believers hungering for God's Word.
4. Pray for protection of house church believers being pressured to join TSPM churches and that they might receive Bibles from the official church without having to register.
5. Pray for revival to enter the hearts of believers in both the TSPM and house churches.

Xian
(shee-ahn)

Meaning: "western peace"
Country: China, Shaanxi Province*
Population: 3,417,000
Poverty: Communism has provided basic needs
Religious Breakdown:
  59.1% Nonreligious/Atheist
  30.1% Chinese Religions
   1.4% Muslim
   6.1% Christian
   5.0% Evangelical
Status of the church: TSPM 113,000 members
Major Religious Sites: Temple of Great
  Maternal Grace, Jianfu Temple, Ba Xian An,
  Big Wild Goose Pagoda, Great Mosque

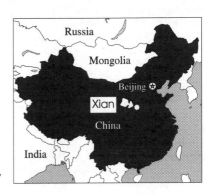

City Significance/History:

Today cities like Beijing and Shanghai are well known to most people. Three thousand years ago Xian was the Rome of the East. Traders came along the Silk Road from Rome, Persia, or Central Asia to do business in this great city. Merchants, artists, and soldiers walked the streets. Priests and emperors were honored and worshiped. The city was the capital for 13 ancient dynasties; as one would fall another would rise. The Silk Road also facilitated the eastward expansion of Buddhism into China.

In the 8th century, 2 million people might have lived in the metro area of Xian. But weakness in the Tang Dynasty permitted Turkish and Tibetan invaders to break up the taxation and wealth base of the dynasty. China was split into independent political states once again. The city declined quickly and never rose to be the national capital again.

The communist government, in its effort to decentralize industry from the eastern mega-cities, has developed Xian into an industrial center. This has resulted in tremendous population growth in the last 50 years, passing its growth in the 8th century. The government has also constructed many grey buildings, turned temples into factories or stores, and greatly improved the railways and roads.

Prayer Points

1. The Nestorian Tablet, the record of Christianity's introduction to China in the 7th century, is housed at the provincial museum. Pray that this stone would speak prophetically to the people regarding their Christian heritage.

2. Pray that in this city of peace the true Prince of Peace might be known.

3. Pray for God's blessing on the unofficial house churches in and around Xian which are training hundreds of evangelists and leaders.

4. Pray that the pioneer church planting efforts of these evangelists throughout central China would be successful.

5. Pray that the city's Muslim quarter might be reached with the gospel.

6. Pray that TSPM members would know Christ as Savior and the Bible as God's Word.

Chengdu
(chung-doo)

Meaning: "perfect city"
Country: China, Sichuan Province *
Population: 3,528,000
Poverty: Rich in agricultural products
Religious Breakdown:
- 59.0% Nonreligious/Atheist
- 30.0% Buddhist/Taoist
- 6.0% Christian
- 1.8% Evangelical

Status of the church: TSPM 55,000 members, 2 churches
Major Religious Sites: Baoguan Monastery, Wenshu Monastery, Marquis Wu Temple, Qingyang Gong Temple (Taoist)

City Significance/History:

Jade and pearls are not the real riches of China—rice, wheat, soybeans, and silk bring the most wealth. Chengdu is the capital of the most populous province, Sichuan, which produces more rice and other grains than any other province. The fertile soil allows for agriculture to play a major role in its livelihood and, of course, silk brought in further wealth.

Du Fu, a bright student, studies to take his college entrance exam. If he makes it into university, he will have a secure future. One of his friends failed the test, not so much because of lack of knowledge, but because of the extreme pressure that rides on this one test.

Du Fu leaves his parent's apartment on the third floor and walks down the poorly lit stairs. Mounting his bike, he heads for Wenshu Monastery. Wenshu is the god of wisdom, and it would be foolish not to offer incense before him. Fighting with other bikes for the right of way, Du Fu makes the left turn leading to Wenshu. He passes the fortune-teller, stopping only briefly to buy incense, then parks his bike.

Finally, before the statue of Buddha that came from Tibet at some earlier date, he lights three sticks of incense and bows gracefully at the waist. The exam grips his mind as he petitions for wisdom.

Prayer Points

1. Many mission agencies are represented here, and each agency has its own view on sharing the gospel. Pray for unity and cooperation between Christians.

2. Pray for the safety of house church believers who face substantial repression from the Religious Affairs Bureau, the TSPM, and police.

3. Pray for an effective witness to Chengdu's "floating population" of migrant laborers from the surrounding villages.

4. Pray for openness among the students interested in books about Christianity.

5. The Marquis Wu Temple holds the history of three gods with one still influencing most Chinese today. Pray that this influence binding the people would be broken.

6. Missionaries and tentmakers here battle loneliness, depression and frustration. Pray for a release from all demonic oppression.

Chongqing
(chong-cheeng)

Day 25

Meaning: "repeated good luck"
Country: China, Sichuan Province
Population: 3,646,000
Poverty: Rich in agricultural products
Religious Breakdown:
    59.1%   Nonreligious/Atheist
    30.1%   Chinese Religions
    1.4%   Muslim
    6.1%   Christian
    5.0%   Evangelical
Status of the church: TSPM 53,00 members
Major Religious Sites: Luo Han Temple,
    Beiwenquan Temple Complex

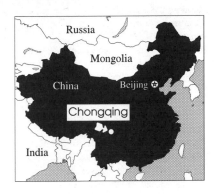

City Significance/History:

Chongqing was established on the peninsula created by the confluence of the Jialing and the Yangtze Rivers. Around 200 B.C., the Ba Kingdom used the peninsula as a capital and important trade center. The peninsula provided natural protection on three sides to resist outside invasion.

The Yangtze River is one of the main arteries across China, and the world's third longest river. The river connects Chongqing to Shanghai. Barges dock at Chaotiamen as dock workers balance bamboo poles on their shoulders to unload the cargo. On the banks of the river, smokestacks spew pollution into the air. Behind the smoke, the hills of the city rise and homes can be seen.

Even though the Japanese heavily bombed the city during World War II, it still retains some of its ancient homes, narrow alleys, and winding stairways. Many refugees from the northeast fled before the murderous Japanese forces as they moved south. The population of Chongqing grew to almost two million.

After the war, peace treaties were signed and the city became the most industrialized city in southwestern China. Industrial growth, a north-south trade location, and a river hub have enabled the city to swell to over 3 million people.

Prayer Points

1. Pray for believers seeking to establish the church in this transportation center, that it would become a hub for spreading the gospel in southwestern China.

2. Chongqing has traditionally been a bastion of Buddhism. Pray that this stronghold would be broken so that the light of the gospel might shine forth.

3. Pray that TSPM members might grow in their walk with the Lord and in their knowledge of the Bible.

4. Pray for workers to reach out to the Tibetans living in Sichuan Province and that Tibetan churches can be established.

5. Pray that worshipers at Luo Han Temple who seek to be released from greed and hate would realize only Christ can forgive sin and give release from condemnation.

Shanghai
(shang-hI)

Meaning: "upper ocean"
Country: China
Population: 15,112,000
Poverty: Rising unemployment
Religious Breakdown:
  59.1%   Nonreligious/Atheist
  27.0%   Buddhist/Taoist
  8.0%   Christian
  2.0%   Evangelical
Status of the church: 80 TSPM churches, TSPM
  headquarters, strong unofficial church
Major Religious Sites: Longhua Temple,
  Temple of Town Gods, Jade Buddha Temple
  1st Communist Party Congress Site

City Significance/History:

Shanghai's strategic location marked this unimportant, small weaving and fishing village as one destined to be China's largest city. The flowing Yangtze River meets the Pacific Ocean just south of Shanghai, connecting the city with far western Tibet and other cities in between. Trading has made it the third largest port in the world.

The British, followed by the French and Japanese, opened the city for their own interests in the 1800s. These foreign entities built autonomous power centers next to each other, in and around Shanghai. With foreign wealth and cheap local labor, the village grew to one million by 1900. The city became very westernized as foreigners built buildings in their own styles. Chinese servants, child-slave labor, and prostitution became part of the imprint of westernization.

After World War II, the communists chose Shanghai to become the first Cultural Revolution "model city." Rehabilitation of opium addicts and the outlawing of child-slave labor credit their efforts.

Overcrowding and unemployment plague the streets. People coming from rural villages are returned because there just is not enough room for them to live and work.

Prayer Points

1. Pray for the university students who seek meaning in life. They willingly listen to the gospel's proclamation and do not resist its truth when they understand it.

2. Prosperity and materialism have gripped the hearts of the people, with money becoming the most important factor in their lives. Pray against this spirit of mammon and greed.

3. Sexual lust and prostitution characterized pre-Revolution Shanghai. These influences are again seeking to undermine the moral fabric of Chinese society. Pray that this spirit of decadence is broken over the city once and for all.

4. Multiple services are required in the official churches to handle the high attendance. Pray that the TSPM churches would become less political and more spiritual.

Wuhan

(wu-**hahn**)

Meaning: names of three cities contracted
Country: China, Hubei Province *
Population: 4,556,000
Poverty: Communism has provided basic needs
Religious Breakdown:
- 59.1%   Nonreligious/Atheist
- 30.1%   Chinese Religions
- 6.1%   Christian
- 5.0%   Evangelical

Status of the church: Many growing TSPM churches, strong house churches
Major Religious Sites:
Guiyuan Temple, Hongshan Pagoda

City Significance/History:

Wuhan's name is a contraction of the names of three cities—Wuchang (Wu), and the names of Hanyang and Hankou (han)—that were finally unified in 1957. Wuchang, on the east bank of the Yangtze River, grew during the Han Dynasty as a regional capital and fortified city.

On the west side of the Yangtze, Hankou was only a village until the city opened for foreign trade. Russians, British, French, Germans, and Japanese set out to establish regional headquarters here. The foreign money turned Hankou into an industrial center in the interior of China. Foreign presence enabled mission agencies to send more workers into the interior. China Inland Mission pioneered the work in Wuhan using both overseas missionaries and national workers.

Next to Hankou, but separated by the smaller Han River, Hanyang had slow beginnings. Hanyang's growth did not come until late in the 19th century, when industrial manufacturers built iron and steel plants. Japan's invasion totally destroyed most of the heavy industry. As rebuilding took place, many of the factories were tooled for light industry.

Today Wuhan is the most important industrial and commercial center in central China.

Prayer Points

1. Pray that TSPM churches like Rong Guang Tang (Glory Church) would be filled with the glory and power of the Lord.

2. Pray for anointed Christian witness to the Chinese military, which has a strong presence in Hubei Province.

3. The province is less than 3% Christian. Pray for the evangelists laboring here and that the Holy Spirit would bring a great harvest.

4. Pray for the effectiveness of foreign Christian professionals teaching in the city and that God would call more teachers willing to endure the hardships of living here in order to have a witness to students.

5. Pray against renewed interest in traditional folk religion and superstitious practices.

Guangzhou
(gwahn-joh)

Meaning: "capital of a large region"
Country: China, Guangdong Province*
Population: 4,184,000
Poverty: Communism has provided basic needs
Religious Breakdown:

59.1%	Nonreligious/Atheist
30.1%	Chinese Religions
6.1%	Christian
5.0%	Evangelical

Status of the church: 15 TSPM churches, growing house churches
Major Religious Sites: Guangxiao Church, Hualin Temple, Wuxian Guan Temple, Six Banyan Trees Temple, Huaishen Mosque

City Significance/History:

Legend tells that the city started after five goats with rice stalks in their mouths descended from heaven. The gods gave the rice and goats as a symbol of freedom from famine, but famines have still come. Guangzhou is also known as Yangcheng, "goat city."

More than any other city in China, Guangzhou (Canton) has been the gateway for trade into China. As early as the second century, traders from the Roman Empire and India came to exchange goods. In the 16th century, Jesuit missionaries established a work in the city. The next few centuries brought more traders and foreign powers to the area. Robert Morrison, the first Protestant missionary, also entered China through Guangzhou in 1807. By the time Mao closed the door to missions, a total of one million Christians were in the province.

Opium became a necessary obsession for the wealthy Chinese. The British brought opium from India to meet the ever-growing demands of the Chinese addicts. The emperor of China finally ordered the city's regional head to get rid of the British. At the conclusion of the Opium War (1839-42), the Chinese surrounded the British, killing many and driving the remaining out of the area—thus ending another violent period.

Prayer Points

1. Pray for the growth and outreach of the harassed house churches such as the well-known 33 Damazhan, and for the safety of their pastors.

2. Ask God to soften the hearts of the Religious Affairs Bureau officials who are antagonistic toward believers who remain outside the TSPM umbrella.

3. Pray that the gospel can be ministered effectively in the midst of social change, economic prosperity, and new ideas and trends flooding in from the outside.

4. Pray that students at the Theological Seminary affiliated with the TSPM Dong Shan Church would be called as pastors and evangelists to the growing church.

5. Children are used as tools for getting money. Pray for these children in bondage to begging. Pray also for the women caught in a life of prostitution.

Hanoi
(ha-**noi**)

Meaning: "the city at the river's bend"
Country: Vietnam*
Population: 1,260,000
Poverty: Poor economy because of war
Religious Breakdown:
   52.0%   Buddhism
   29.8%   Nonreligious/Atheist
   3.0%   Animist
   9.8%   Christian (mainly Catholic)
   0.78%   Evangelical
Status of the church: Small but growing
Major Religious Sites: Chua Mot Cot (One
   Pillar Pagoda), Dien Huu Pagoda, Quan Su
   Pagoda, Ho Chi Minh Mausoleum

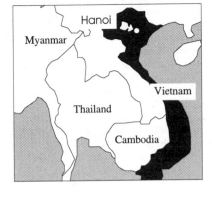

City Significance/History:

For 1000 years, Hanoi has housed emperors and government officials. Under the Emperor Ly Thai To, the site was known as Souring Dragon. By the 20th century, the French ruled Indochina from their regional capital at Hanoi. The French colonial period inspired many Vietnamese to desire a free and independent homeland. The French suppressed a number of uprisings, but Marxist-Leninist revolutionary theory was taking root among the educated.

During World War II power control of Indochina changed from France to Japan, while the Communist Party grew in northern Vietnam. The following years saw the Vietnamese communists take power, dividing the country between north and south in civil war. This war escalated into the Vietnam War, where cities and villages of civilians were destroyed to kill a few of the enemy's forces. In the end, the communist north gained control of the whole country. Slowly the civil war gave rise to peace under communism.

Four decades of suffering have started to allow greater freedom for a market economy. Religious figures (Buddhist and Catholic) have been imprisoned in recent years because they represented voices against communist oppression.

Prayer Points

1. Pray that restrictions on the importation of Bibles will be removed.

2. Pressure by security forces on unregistered churches is growing. The government officially has loosened its rigid grip on religion, but police continue to raid churches. Pray for believers to have freedom to worship without harassment.

3. As business relations normalize with the outside world, pray for tentmakers to be called to work in the city.

4. Pray for a new generation of pastors to be raised up, and that the study materials and books needed to train them will become available.

5. Pray that the strongholds of communism and Buddhism would yield to the power of the Holy Spirit.

Vientiane
(vyen-**tyahn**)

Meaning: "city of the moon"
Country: Laos*
Population: 491,000
Poverty: Subsistence economy
Religious Breakdown:

- 58.7%   Buddhism
- 33.0%   Animist
- 5.1%   Nonreligious/Atheist
- 1.53%   Christian (mainly Catholic)
- 0.72%   Evangelical

Status of the church: Steadily growing
Major Religious Sites: Great Sacred Stupa,
Wat Si Muang, Wat Ong Teu Mahawihan,
Wat Sok Pa Luang, Wat Si Saket

City Significance/History:

The Mekong River and fertile plains made Vientiane a natural site for the Lao people to settle and start a small kingdom. Tradition tells that the city was established in the 16th century, when Wat Si Muang's pillar was laid.

Buddhist religious leaders wanted to build a new wat (sacred place where monks live) with a stone pillar as the centerpiece and Buddhas surrounding. A hole was dug, a rope balanced the selected stone pillar above it; however, a sacrifice was needed. Gongs called the villagers to the site. Whether voluntary or not, a pregnant woman jumped into the

A sacrifice was needed

hole and was crushed under the heavy pillar. The temple's name means "sacred city."

The lack of military power allowed the area to be overrun by every neighboring empire. The Thai, Chinese, Vietnamese, and later French, Americans, and Russians all left their mark on the city. Since the 16th century, it has been a capital, but as early as the 2nd century Buddhist monks passed this way.

For the last 30 years, the communists have held power. Even though most of the country is very fertile, Laos has an extremely poor standard of living.

Prayer Points

1. The church suffered much under communism, with many believers falling away or backsliding. Pray for reconciliation and unity in the body of Christ.

2. Pray that all restrictions against public evangelism, church building, and missionaries will be lifted.

3. Pray for the tentmakers working in the city and that opportunities to present the gospel would arise.

4. Most of the church's trained leaders left in 1975. Pray for national pastors and teachers to be equipped and that training materials would become available.

5. Pray that the resurgence of Buddhism would be countered with the gospel.

Phnom Penh
(nom pen)

Day 27

Meaning: "the hill of a woman named Penh"
Country: Cambodia (Kampuchea)*
Population: 2,827,000
Poverty: War caused economic devastation
Religious Breakdown:
  87.0% Buddhist
  7.8% Nonreligious/Atheist
  2.7% Animist
  0.38% Christian (mainly Catholic)
  0.08% Evangelical
Status of the church: 30 congregations
Major Religious Sites: Wat Phnom, Silver
  Pagoda, Wat Qunalom Monastery, Nur
  ul-Ihsan Mosque, Independence Monument

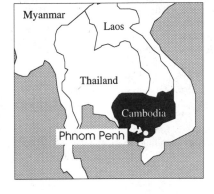

City Significance/History:

In the mid-15th century, the Khmer people were fighting the Thai, a long-standing enemy like the Vietnamese. The Thai captured the city of Angkor, causing the Khmer to relocate to Phnom Penh. Over 100 years earlier, Penh had found a Buddha in one of the three rivers that run through the area. She placed the Buddha on the highest hill as a holy pagoda.

Battles with the Thai and Vietnamese continued, along with occupations by the Spanish and French. Catholic monks arrived with the Westerners.

Slowly the communist Khmer Rouge started to take over rural areas. By the 1960s they controlled provincial capitals, and in 1975 Phnom Penh fell into their hands. Being communist, they wanted to rid the country of all religion. Buddhist monks were killed, and of the estimated 10,000 Christians in Phnom Penh the vast majority were stabbed to death. The Khmer Rouge killed many people, including the educated, because they wanted to "purify" the Khmer people from outside influence.

The Vietnamese, because of border battles, sent troops into Phnom Penh. In 1979 the Khmer Rouge finally fell. The United Nations, in recent years, has tried to reestablish peace.

Prayer Points

1. Pray for unity among the local church leaders as well as the Christian leaders from other countries who work in Phnom Penh.

2. Pray for protection of the body of Christ from materialism, corruption, wrong doctrine, and competition.

3. Pray that God will raise up more Christian leaders to disciple the harvest that is pouring into the kingdom of God. Youth workers are needed particularly.

4. Pray that God will grant wisdom and finance to Christians who are willing to pioneer practical projects to rebuild the city and the lives of the people.

5. Many innocent people were tortured by the Khmer Rouge in prisons like Tuol Sleng. Pray for healing of the victims and forgiveness for former enemies.

Bangkok
(bang-kok)

Meaning: "city of angels, home of all the gods"
Country: Thailand*
Population: 8,627,000
Poverty: Some slum communities
Religious Breakdown:

   93.4% Buddhist
   4.0% Muslim
   2.7% Animist
   1.0% Christian
   0.3% Evangelical

Status of the church: Very slow growth
Major Religious Sites: Wat Arun,
City Pillar Shrine, Reclining Buddha Temple,
Golden Buddha Temple, Marble Temple,
Emerald Buddha Temple, Wat Saket

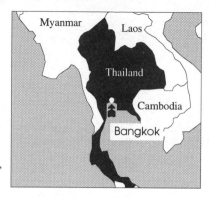

City Significance/History:

Bangkok (Krung Thep) began as a small village by the Chao Phya River in the 18th century, and later became the capital of Thailand. Now over 8 million people make their home in the vast sprawl of waterways and streets of Bangkok. Its amazing growth is due primarily to the heavy influx of poor rural migrants.

Buddhism, with endless cycles of reincarnation, teaches people to perform religious rituals to gain merit, hopefully earning a better go-round in the next life. Behind Buddhism is a complex world of Hindu gods and venerated spirits. In daily crises and fears, the people of Bangkok turn to the spirit world, superstition, and astrology. Spirit houses stand in front of homes to keep the evil spirits outside. Many people wear amulets thought to contain spiritual powers.

The City Pillar Shrine, thought to be inhabited by the city's guardian spirit, was inspired by the Hindu custom of centrally placing a phallic symbol in Shiva temples. This ruling spirit is perhaps why Bangkok is known for its night life. The prostitution rings have been pulling village girls and boys away from their homes—exploiting them until they are too old or have contracted AIDS—which is a growing epidemic.

Prayer Points

1. The prostitution rings have grown and the AIDS epidemic has increased. Without the closing down of these financially prosperous rings, the situation will just deteriorate. Ask God to completely shut down this illicit activity.

2. AIDS will have an inevitable impact on leadership in coming generations, even in the church. Pray that the spread of this epidemic can be stopped.

3. Pray that the many street children may be reached with the gospel and that child slavery will end.

4. Pray for biblical teaching to counter the influence of other religions and cults.

5. The lure of materialism is infecting the church. Pray that a biblical perspective on money and stewardship will come

Yangon

(**yen**-gen)

Meaning: "no more enemy"
Country: Myanmar*
Population: 3,905,000
Poverty: Poorest country in Asia,
22.6% inflation
Religious Breakdown:
  89.0% Buddhist
  4.0% Muslim
  4.0% Christian
  2.5% Evangelical
Status of the church: Both an "official" and
an unregistered church
Major Religious Sites: Shwedagon Pagoda,
Kaba Aye Pagoda, Innwa Jail, Sule Pagoda

City Significance/History:

Some 500 years before Christ, the Mon people established their empire at this location. Having close relations with Indian kings allowed Buddhism to spread quickly among the Mons. It was on the Singuttara Hill where they chose to build the Shwedagon Pagoda. Buddhist tradition tells that five lotus flowers gave rise to five birds, each carrying a yellow robe or wrap. The robes were for five Buddhas that would reach enlightenment and then guide this world to Nirvana. So far, four of the five Buddhas have appeared. When the fifth, Maitreya, appears he will bring the new world cycle. Each of the past four Buddhas have left relics (a staff, filter for water, one of the robes, and eight head hairs) all at Shwedagon.

Throughout history, pilgrims have come to this pagoda, bringing their offerings and hoping for Nirvana to come quickly. The high place of the hilltop pagoda made it strategic.

The British, in their quest to control more trade in the east, captured Shwedagon because it overlooked the delta below. The city developed under the British. When the Japanese arrived, they were viewed as liberators from the British rule. Shortly after World War II, the country was granted independence.

Prayer Points

1. Pray for unity between the denominational and evangelical churches.

2. Pray that the church leaders would grow in their vision for the local church, and that the local church would reach out in Jesus' name.

3. Pray for Christian leadership training and other short-term training programs—for more local leaders to move the gospel forward.

4. Pray that the government would change its authoritarian policies.

5. It is very difficult to evangelize Buddhists. Pray that the spiritual strongholds over Buddhism would be broken down.

6. Pray for the poor—that their physical needs would be met and that they would have the good news preached to them.

Dhaka
(dah-kuh)

Meaning: after Durga, wife of Shiva
Country: Bangladesh*
Population: 9,105,000
Poverty: Many slum areas
Religious Breakdown:
   87.0%   Muslim
   11.7%   Hindu
    0.7%   Buddhist
    0.44% Christian
    0.08% Evangelical
Status of the church: Slow, steady growth
Major Religious Sites: Hassain Dolan
   Mosque, Baitul Mukarram Mosque,
   Kashaitully Mosque, Holy Resurrection
   Armenian Church

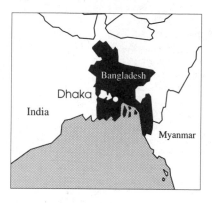

City Significance/History:

Dhaka was established at its present site in the 4th century because of the agricultural wealth along the Burigange River.

Because of the flooded coastal deltas and the Chittagong Hills, the majority of the population lives in the central plains.

Few outsiders ventured to this isolated city until, in the mid-18th century, the Mongol Empire extended its borders once again, this time including Bengal. Dhaka became a regional capital.

When the British entered the Indian subcontinent, Bengal came under their authority. After independence in 1971, the country went through a civil war and emerged as Bangladesh. The population has continued to explode.

Famines and natural disasters have plagued the country and city, keeping poverty high. Many people from all regions have relocated to Dhaka hoping for a better life. The old section of Dhaka, called Sadarghat, has been a growing slum that provides few opportunities for the poor to improve their lot. The stagnation of the economy has seen even the educated fall into poverty. The government is setting up programs to help the poor. The poor can receive government loans with no interest for the establishment of small businesses.

Prayer Points

1. Pray that the government's increasingly restrictive laws against Christians will be modified, and that extremist Muslim groups will not prevail.

2. Pray for an increased response to the gospel from Muslims and that church leaders coming from a Muslim background will have the strength to persevere and to withstand persecution.

3. The Great Commission Movement was launched in 1991 to plant churches and reach ethnic groups. Pray that its goals would be reached and for the church to grow.

4. Pray that Christian media, literature, and Bibles would continue to reap a harvest and that the demand can be met.

5. Nearly 40 students at the university have died because of student gang warfare. Pray that the Prince of Peace might be known on campus.

Kuala Lumpur
(kwah-luh luum-poor)

Day 29

Meaning: "muddy river confluence"
Country: Malaysia
Population: 1,800,000
Poverty: 36% of population is poor
Religious Breakdown:
  34.2%   Muslim
  30.9%   Buddhist
  17.7%   Chinese Religions
  10.2%   Hindu
  4.5%   Christian
Status of the church: 113 churches
Major Religious Sites: Masjid Jame Mosque, Masjid Negara Mosque, Shah Alam Mosque, Sri Mamariamman Temple, International Buddhist Pagoda, Batu Caves (Hindu)

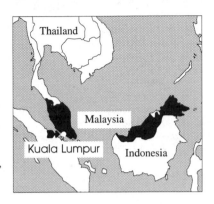

City Significance/History

Prospecting for tin brought an influx of people in 1857 to where the Klang and Gombak rivers converge. Soon after tin was found, Kuala Lumpur became a boom town. People came from as far as China to mine tin.

The city never looked back. It has grown to be the capital and largest city of Malaysia— a cultural hub and business center, particularly for the rubber and tin industries. The make-up of Kuala Lumpur includes Chinese, Indian (brought in by the British to work the rubber plantations), and the ethnic Malay.

These three groups have vastly different religious beliefs (Buddhism, Hinduism, and Islam). Yet in a region most often associated with Buddhism and animism, the Malays stand out as a strong Islamic force. To be Malay is to be Muslim. For a Malay to become a Christian means to leave his or her cultural roots.

The government has closed the doors for Christian outreach to Malays, but there are no restrictions on witnessing to non-Malays. It is illegal for anyone to proselytize the ethnic Malay. For Christians to reach out to Malays means prosecution and even imprisonment.

Prayer Points

1. Pray against a spirit of superstition among the Malays, who employ the service of the local *bomoh*, "spirit magician," to deal with spiritual issues. Pray that God will continue to reveal himself through dreams and visions.

2. Divorce is a common element in Malay society because of a lack of trust in many marriages. Pray for the establishment of Christian ministries to answer this problem.

3. Pray that government restrictions against evangelizing the Malays will be lifted— that persecution of Malay converts and believers who witness to them will cease.

4. Pray that household evangelism to Buddhists and Hindus will bear much fruit.

5. Pray for unity in the church, despite persecution, and that God would strengthen the pastors and leaders.

Jakarta
(juh-**kahr**-tuh)

Day 29

Meaning: "place of victory"
Country: Indonesia*
Population: 11,401,000
Poverty: 15% of population is poor
Religious Breakdown:
  96.0%   Muslim
   3.6%   Christian
   1.4%   Evangelical
Status of the church: Growth in recent years
Major Religious Sites: Istiqlal Mosque,
  Al Azhar Mosque, Vihara Dharama Jaya
  Temple, Wisma Subud Cilandak
  Headquarters, Gerja Sion Church

City Significance/History:

Hindu travelers found the port of Sunda Kelapa in Jakarta useful for protection from storms and a good trade center. Control by the Hindu powers passed to traders from the northern islands who brought Islam. By the 16th century, European forces were vying for control of the wealth and trade. The British and Dutch both set up trading posts; however, it was the Dutch who finally established a fort and gained control of the area. It became their hub for administration in all of the East Indies.

At the end of World War II, Jakarta was freed from Japanese domination, and it became the capital of the independent country of Indonesia. The abortive communist coup in 1965 produced much bloodshed.

As the country's population exploded in the last fifty years, Jakarta has become a modern city with tremendous slums. The arrival of villagers, due to economically depressed rural areas, pushed the slums to over 60% of the city's population in the early 1970s. Shantytowns have been hid behind modern buildings, and the government has been relocating many of the poor to other islands. Today the poverty rate is about 15% in the city.

Prayer Points

1. Pray that the government will promote the development of a pluralistic nation in which all religions have full freedom of worship.

2. Pray for the development of democracy and that the process of succession scheduled for 1998 will be smooth and accepted by the major political forces.

3. Pray that the process of modernization will not destroy traditional family life.

4. Pray that God will use the press and electronic media as a means to glorify his name—that Christian programming would be abundant.

5. Pray for the continued growth of the church and for mature leaders to lead the new believers in truth.

6. Pray that the rise of Islam will be countered with the truth of the gospel.

Bandar Seri Begawan
(bend-er ser-ee beg-uh-wun)

Day 29

Meaning: unknown
Country: Brunei*
Population: 110,000
Poverty: Oil produced wealth
Religious Breakdown:

71.0%	Muslim
9.0%	Chinese Religions
6.5%	Nonreligious
3.7%	Animist
8.0%	Christian
1.0%	Evangelical

Status of the church: A few Chinese small fellowships, no known Malay believers
Major Religious Sites: Omar Ali Saifuddin Mosque, Tomb of Sultan Bolkiah

Bandar Seri Begawan

Brunei

Malaysia

Indonesia

City Significance/History:

Located at the mouth of the Brunei River and protected by the Brunei Bay, Bandar Seri Begawan has been a seat of power for the control of northern Borneo to the Philippines. The city overlooks the bay where European ships would rest and seek trade. But with time, the power of the sultan in the area declined and pirates began to prey on European trade ships as they passed.

Islam entered the country in the 15th century through the conversion of Sultan Awang Alak Beter. He was a pagan ruler until he heard about Islam, probably through Muslim traders. To show his desire to be identified with Islam, he changed his name to Sultan Muhammad, after the founder of Islam.

The British had developed strong trade routes between China, India, and England. Piracy was something they could not allow. The British captured the area in the early 19th century, making the country a British protectorate until 1983. Oil was found off the coast 50 years ago. The wealth of the city again grew.

The current sultan, reportedly the world's richest man, represents one of the oldest, continuously ruling dynasties in the world. Oil has made Brunei one of the wealthiest nations in Asia.

Prayer Points

1. Pray that Christian literature may be imported and that contact with foreign Christians be allowed.

2. Pray that evangelism may be allowed legally among the Muslims.

3. Pray that the government leaders will provide constitutional protection to Christians and allow for public celebration of Christmas.

4. Sultan Beter turned the whole country towards Islam. Pray that God would soften the heart of the current sultan and allow his nation to turn to Christ.

5. Pray for disillusionment with the materialism brought by oil money and that the people would desire true riches in Jesus Christ.

Ulaanbaatar
(oo-lahn-**bah**-tor)

Day 30

Meaning: "red warrior"
Country: Mongolia*
Population: 600,000
Poverty: 26.5% of population is poor.
Religious Breakdown:
    50.0%   Shamanist/Animist
    26.0%   Buddhist
    19.0%   Nonreligious
    4.0%   Muslim
    0.03% Christian
Status of the church: 10 churches
Major Religious Sites: Gandan Monastery,
    Mongolian Astrologers Center

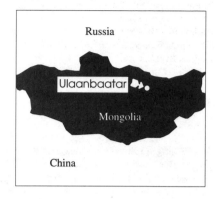

City Significance/History:

The Gobi Desert and steppes of the Mongolian flatlands have historically produced warriors that have conquered vast territories. The Great Wall of China was built to keep the Mongols out. (The wall never physically failed; it was the watchtower guards being bribed that allowed the Mongols through.) Central Asia and Persia saw the Mongols sweep through. The great unifier of the Mongols, Genghis Khan ("universal king") expanded the Mongol Empire to Arabia, Russia, and China.

In the 17th century Ulaanbaatar became the home of Jebtsundamba Hutuktu, one of the revelations of the living Buddha. Almost 100 years later, Gandan Monastery was built in the city as a Buddhist center and temple.

With the fall of the Mongolian Empire, Mongolia became a territory fought over between China and Russia, at times controlled by one or the other power.

Stalin, in the 1930s, shut down the monasteries and imprisoned the monks because they were too powerful. Commuism fell apart in Mongolia in 1990 and religion was able to reestablish itself. Gandan is now the only functioning monastery in the country; the rest have been closed or turned into museums.

Prayer Points

1. Continuing economic difficulties and unemployment make life hard for Mongol families. Pray that the hardships these people are going through would be alleviated.

2. The city council is requiring churches to register and give the name, gender, work place, and address of all members. Pray that believers can freely meet and worship, and for the raising up of Mongol leaders to guide the new fellowships.

3. Disunity among Christians exists over which Mongolian Bible version is preferable. Pray for consensus on this important issue. Some short-term missionaries have been counter-productive in their witness. Pray for wisdom for those working in the city.

4. Pray that cults and other religions would not confuse the young believers and that the false religions would decrease in popularity.

Pyongyang
(pyung-yahng)

Meaning: "peaceful ocean"
Country: North Korea*
Population: 2,471,000
Poverty: Rationing of basic foodstuffs
Religious Breakdown:

    68.0%   Nonreligious/Atheist
    29.5%   Korean Religions
    1.7%   Buddhist
    0.6%   Christian
    0.36% Evangelical

Status of the church: 3 official churches, numerous house churches
Major Religious Sites: Tower of the Juche Idea, Manyongdae Monument (Sung's birthplace)

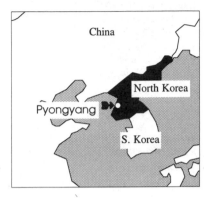

City Significance/History:

Since 2333 B.C., Pyongyang has been central for powers ruling the Korean peninsula. The Chinese, Japanese, and the Wang Dynasty all tried to control it. Few Western ideas penetrated the area, but Roman Catholicism did. The farmers followed this new religion. Because they were uneducated and poor, the government paid little attention until some Confucian aristocrats converted.

By the 19th century, Christian missionaries were sailing up the Taedong River to Pyongyang. The Confucian government attacked and sank one ship. Robert Thomas escaped by swimming to shore. Before he was martyred, he presented a Bible to his executioners. The killing of over 8000 Korean Catholics and the few Protestants followed.

In 1930 Pyongyang, with its many churches, was considered Asia's capital of Christianity. However, in 1945 before the Japanese surrendered, Stalin placed troops in northern Korea. The Communist regime that emerged was led by Kim II Sung. Thousands of Christians were martyred during and after the Korean War. In recent years Billy Graham has visited Pyongyang and shared the gospel with the late President Kim. This Marxist nation remains one of the most closed countries to Christianity.

Prayer Points

1. Pray that the government in transition will change its policy and allow religious freedom, true public worship, and the construction of church buildings.

2. Pray that the house churches would be given growth, opportunity, and freedom to develop into mature congregations. Pray for Christian leaders to be raised up.

3. Pray that believers could be contacted and visited by Christians from the outside and that they could travel to international gatherings.

4. Currently the official church is not allowed to cooperate with outsiders in Bible distribution. Pray that Bibles and other Christian literature can be produced, especially for school children. Pray that a press to print Bibles can be established.

5. Pray for national reunification between the South and North. South Korean Christians greatly desire to spread their spiritual fervor northward.

Sapporo
(suh-**poor**-oh)

Day 30

Meaning: "dry, big river"
Country: Japan, Hokkaido*
Population: 2,300,000
Poverty: Very little
Religious Breakdown:
    90.0%   Buddhist/Shintoist
     8.0%   Atheist
     1.0%   Christian
     0.5%   Evangelical
Status of the church: 113 indigenous churches
    starting new churches themselves
Major Religious Sites:
    Hokkaido Jingu Shrine

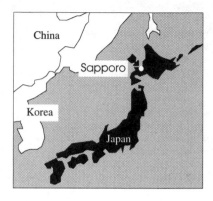

City Significance/History:

Sapporo developed as a small Ainu village. The Ainu were a distinct people from the Japanese, but would interact with them in trade. The Ainu traded bear meat and salmon for cloth and iron goods.

The Iyomante Festival was the climax of the bear worship, one of the animal god/spirits they worshiped. The spirits of the animals were central to their lives. And Ainu women would raise (including breast feeding) a bear cub in honor to the animal. The fur and meat of the bear was extremely important to life, and each animal received prayers of thanksgiving and requests for the animal's afterlife.

As the number of Japanese increased, the islands to the south needed more land. The outnumbered Ainu people were crushed and forced to move north by the advancing Japanese. The northern island of Hokkaido fell to the Japanese in the mid-19th century, and Sapporo was then established as their territorial capital in 1869.

In the last one hundred years, the city has grown to be the island's cultural, political, and economic center. In 1972 the Winter Olympics were held here. Ainu culture has mostly disappeared, as the two groups have intermarried.

Prayer Points

1. Pray for unity within the churches—that through cooperation evangelistic outreaches would be extremely effective, and for wisdom in planting new churches.

2. Most homes have a *Butsudan* (Buddhist family altar) for the worship of ancestors. Pray that the generational hold of these family altars would be broken.

3. Pray that the spirit of materialism over the city would be overthrown.

4. Hokkaido has the highest rate of divorce in Japan. Pray that family life will be strengthened and families reconciled through Christ.

5. Pray for believers as they continue to evangelize their neighbors and friends.

6. Pray that the animistic beliefs of the Ainu would be broken and that the strained relationships between the native Ainu and the Japanese will be healed.

Tokyo-Yokohama

Day 31

(**toh**-ki-oh/**yoh**-kuh-**hah**-ma)

Meaning: Tokyo*—"eastern capital,"
Yokohama—"by the beach"
Country: Japan
Population: 18,527,000
Poverty: Little poverty
Religious Breakdown:
  99.0% Shintoist & Buddhist
  1.0% Christian
  0.25% Evangelical
Status of the church: T—922, Y—465
Major Religious Sites: T—Yasukuni and
  Meiji Shrines, Kwannon and Kaneiji Temples;
  Y—Asakusa Amanawa Shrines,
  Great Buddha Statue, Hasedera Temple

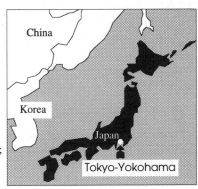

City Significance/History:

About 500 years ago, fishers and rice farmers lived in the small village of Edo. Three rivers joined there, but very little took place in this sleepy village. A fort was built in the mid-16th century to protect the military Shogun (Takugawa) capital. With time, the marshy lowlands were reclaimed and the city expanded. The Shogun rule turned Japan's economy from the wealth of the aristocracy into a commercial state. Edo continued to grow and develop, until the 18th century when it hit one million people—the largest city of the time.

As Edo grew, foreigners desired greater contact with the city. The Takugawa government did not want the foreigners in Edo, so they allowed the fishing settlement of Yokohama to house the international community. The development of this port city allowed for foreign trade and technology to increase throughout Japan. Industries were built and the city grew.

Today Tokyo and Yokohama make up one of the greatest metropolitan mega-cities in the world. The population has continued to increase and more land has been reclaimed from rivers and the ocean. Tokyo is home to the Japanese Parliament and the powerful Ministry of International Trade and Industry.

Prayer Points

1. Pray for God to shake the city and nation. The biggest barrier to the gospel is a sense that it is irrelevant to people, as almost all are materially satisfied. A spirit of materialism motivates this global economic center.

2. Pray against the rise and influence of cults like Mormons, Jehovah's Witnesses, and Moonies, as well as new Buddhist-influenced religious movements.

3. Pray for the salvation of the Imperial family and that official visits to the Yasokuni Shrine by politicians will be discontinued.

4. Pray for unity and mutual understanding between non-charismatic and charismatic Christians. Suspicion has led to lack of cooperation and spiritual pride.

5. Pray for Japanese believers to engage in personal evangelism and not just invite friends to church meetings—this could lead to significant church growth.

Osaka-Kobe-Kyoto

(oh-**sah**-kuh/**koh**-bee/kee-**oh**-toh)

Day 31

Meaning: O—"large slope"
Ko—"door of the gods"
Ky—"capital city"
Country: Japan
Population: 8,563,000
Poverty: Little poverty
Religious Breakdown:
97.5%   Shintoist & Buddhist
2.5%   Christian
0.32%   Evangelical
Status of the church: O-522, Ko-405, Ky-193
Major Religious Sites: O—Shitennoji Temple,
Sumiyoshi and Temmangu Shrines; Ko—Ikuta-
jinja Shrine; Ky—Daitokuji and Ryoanji
Temples, Kibone Shrine

City Significance/History:

Shitennoji Temple was built in Osaka back in the 6th century. Tradition states the temple was constructed by Prince Shotoku when he vowed to build it during the heat of a battle to the Shitenno (the four gods who protect the cardinal points of the compass). Osaka had grown and become a center for the Isiyama Honganji. This religious and secular organization built a temple fortress at nearby Kyoto that attracted pilgrims.

From 794–1869 Kyoto was the capital of Japan, a religious monarchy at the time. The rise of the Shogun power in Edo (Tokyo) saw the area lose importance to the northern capital. Today Kyoto is the national center of culture and Buddhism, where over 2000 temples and shrines exist. The city recently celebrated its 1200th anniversary.

Osaka Bay was large and protected, a great location for trade with the outside world. In 1868 Commodore Perry forced open the port at Kobe, and foreign trade flourished with few restrictions. This freedom caused the port to expand while Osaka's population growth allowed the two cities to unite.

Industry, business, and international trade have caused the three cities to form the Keihanshin Industrial Zone.

Prayer Points

1. As a pilgrimage site, Kyoto draws over 1/3 of the Japanese people yearly. Pray that these pilgrims would seek the truth of God through Christ.

2. Pray that the emphasis on prayer, created during the Koshien Crusade of 1993, will continue to be a focal point in the life of the church.

3. Pray against a sense of national pride that makes people feel, "I'm Japanese, so I don't need a foreign religion like Christianity."

4. Pray that Kobe can rebuild after its devastating earthquake and that people will seek God for comfort and strength.

5. Pray for believers to have a greater awareness of evil spirits and occultism and their spiritual effect in people's lives.

Fukuoko-Kita-Kyushu

Day 31 (**foo**-koo-**oh**-koh/**kee**-tuh/**kee-oo**-shoo)

Meaning: F — "blessed hill,"
  KK — "north nine states"
Country: Japan
Population: 4,164,000
Poverty: Little poverty
Religious Breakdown:
  95.0% Shintoist & Buddhist
  2.5% Christian
  0.32% Evangelical
Status of the church: F-85; KK-72
Major Religious Sites: KK—Sumiyoshi Shrine,
  F—Shofukuji Temple, Kushida Shrine,
  Munaga Taisha Shrine, Dazaifu Tenmangu
  Shrine, Aso Mountain

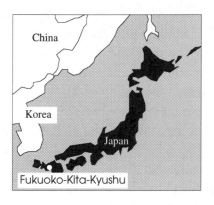

City Significance/History:

As early as 300 B.C., a fort was located at Hakata Bay. This small community traded with Korea and other lands, but was not a power in the area.

In the late 6th century, Fukuoko became the primary city for trade with China. Hakata Bay provided great protection from the ocean, and its location just off of Korea made it a natural springboard for trade with China.

The trade routes brought Zen (deep meditative) Buddhism to Japan in the 12th century. Today the Shofukuji Temple stands as the oldest Zen temple in Japan.

One hundred years later, Mongol invaders twice tried to conquer Japan through Hakata Bay. The invasions were not successful, more because of violent typhoons than the Japanese superiority in fighting. Japan was saved from the well-trained Mongol forces.

By this century, the city became an industrial and fishing center. It was the largest city on the island of Kyushu, as well as the political center.

In 1963 five cities of Fukuoko province were incorporated to form Kita-Kyushu. This united city is now the island's most important industrial center. The local government desires to increase foreign trade and to become Japan's gateway to the rest of Asia.

Prayer Points

1. Pray for revival motivated by a spirit of repentance, and that joy and enthusiasm might replace the formality in worship services.

2. Pray that seminaries will teach sound biblical theology, so that new graduates will be empowered to lead the church into spiritual growth. Pray for encouragement and spiritual strength for the pastors, that they might be refreshed by the Holy Spirit.

3. Pray that the grip of juvenile delinquency upon the area will be broken, and that the Christians ministering to these youth can lead them to the Lord.

4. Pray against occultism and false religions, which are especially targeting the youth.

5. Pray that the churches will be an example of cooperation in evangelism.

Resource Directory

Books

Listed below are several books to assist you in praying more knowledgeably and effectively for the 100 Gateway Cities. They may be purchased at your local Christian bookstore or ordered directly from the United Prayer Track by calling 818-577-5599. To receive a copy of *The Arsenal,* a resource guide on prayer and spiritual warfare, write Global Harvest Ministries, 215 North Marengo Ave., Suite 151, Pasadena, CA 91101.

Taking Our Cities for God by John Dawson.
A formative work on how God loves and wants to redeem our cities through prayer and healing.

The Jericho Hour by Dick Eastman.
A strategic book on spiritual warfare's role in fulfilling the Great Commission. Practical examples and inspiring teaching.

Love on Its Knees: Make A Difference by Praying for Others by Dick Eastman.
Principles of intercession to help you pray with dramatic effectiveness for unknown people in foreign lands, as well as for your own loved ones.

Prayer-Walking: Praying On Site With Insight by Steve Hawthorne and Graham Kendrick.
Ordinary believers are stepping into the streets to pray effectively for their neighbors. This is a practical menu of proven ideas to begin preparing whole cities for spiritual awakening.

Possessing the Gates of the Enemy by Cindy Jacobs.
A guide for those wanting to join the battle of spiritual warfare. Definitively describes the gift of intercession and how to know in what direction you may be called to be an intercessor.

Operation World: Day to Day Guide to Praying For the World by Patrick Johnstone.
To help individuals and groups to more effectively intercede for the world, it includes comprehensive information, accurate statistics, and detailed maps and graphs.

The Last of the Giants: Lifting the Veil on Islam and the End Time by George Otis, Jr.
Takes the reader on a "behind the scenes" journey into understanding the major spiritual forces in the world today — Islam, Hinduism, and materialism.

Breaking Strongholds in your City edited by C. Peter Wagner
The first textbook on spiritual mapping for the average Christian. Contributors include George Otis, Jr., Cindy Jacobs, Kjell Sjoberg, and others.

Churches that Pray by C. Peter Wagner
How prayer relates to the growth of the local church and why it is necessary to pray not only in the church but also in the community.

Engaging the Enemy edited by C. Peter Wagner
18 prayer leaders share practical spiritual warfare experience.

Prayer Shield by C. Peter Wagner
How to intercede for pastors, Christian leaders, and others on the spiritual frontlines with excellent material for intercessors.

Warfare Prayer by C. Peter Wagner.
How to seek God's power and protection in the battle to build his kingdom. This widely acclaimed book will guide everyone who wants to join the battle of spiritual warfare.

Tapes

A video called *Light The Window* is available which depicts the spiritual need in the 10/40 Window. It tells the story of how God is using the global prayer movement through Praying Through the Window to fulfill the Great Commission in this last frontier of world evangelization.

Audio teaching tapes with additional information on the 100 Gateway Cities are also available. These were recorded at several conferences held to train prayer journeyers to pray on site in these cities. The tapes are full of practical information on how to have a successful prayer journey.

To order these tapes, contact the Christian Information Network, 11025 State Highway 83, Colorado Springs, CO 80921; phone (719) 522-1040; fax (719) 548-9000.

Prayer Calendars

Prayer calendars for Praying Through the Window II are also available from the Christian Information Network.

Prayer Books

Additional copies of *Praying Through the 100 Gateway Cities of the 10/40 Window* may be obtained from your local Christian bookstore or ordered directly from the Christian Information Network.